Praise for

Hallelujah! The Welcome Table

"Now the truth is evident: Poet and literary legend Maya Angelou is as mighty with her spoon and spatula as she is with her world-renowned pen."
—*Chicago Sun-Times*

"*Hallelujah! The Welcome Table*—a cookbook in a sense that there are recipes—is the poet's life laid out like a colorful banquet." —*Milwaukee Journal Sentinel*

"Warning: Don't read Maya Angelou's new book while hungry.... This cookbook is a tour-de-force collaboration of two of Angelou's major passions—writing and cooking."
—*Ebony*

"Readers of this ███ will █████ ██ ████████ of █████ ███████ allow them to set aside their o██████ ███ ██████ ████ ███ █████ ███ ████ ████ ██ cakes, pies and fried chicken, b█████ ████ ███ ██████ ██████ ███ ███ █████ writer and her family."
███ ████ ████ ███ ██ ████ ████ ██ ███ ███ ████ ██rk *Daily News*

"Poet Maya Ang██████ ███ ███ ██████ ███ ████ ██ █████ ███ stories . . . an evocative work."
████ ████ ███ ███ ████ ███ ███ ███ ████ ███ ███ ██cisco *Chronicle*

"It is not surprising when a culinary life is played out in the pages of a book with recipes. But when the life of a poet-autobiographer, already revealed through verse and narrative, comes even more alive through plumes of aromas, a palette of flavors and a recipe box of memories, a cookbook is something else."
—*Seattle Post-Intelligencer*

"*Hallelujah! The Welcome Table* is more than a collection of printed recipes . . . it's a humorous and poignant memoir graced by g█

Also by Maya Angelou

Autobiography

I Know Why the Caged Bird Sings

Gather Together in My Name

*Singin' and Swingin' and
Gettin' Merry Like Christmas*

The Heart of a Woman

*All God's Children
Need Traveling Shoes*

A Song Flung Up to Heaven

Essays

*Wouldn't Take Nothing for
My Journey Now*

Even the Stars Look Lonesome

Poetry

*Just Give Me a Cool Drink
of Water 'fore I Diiie*

*Oh Pray My Wings Are
Gonna Fit Me Well*

And Still I Rise

Shaker, Why Don't You Sing?

I Shall Not Be Moved

On the Pulse of Morning

Phenomenal Woman

*The Complete Collected Poems
of Maya Angelou*

A Brave and Startling Truth

Amazing Peace

Mother

Celebrations

Children's Books

*My Painted House,
My Friendly Chicken, and Me*

Kofi and His Magic

Picture Books

Now Sheba Sings the Song

Life Doesn't Frighten Me

Hallelujah!
The
Welcome
Table

Hallelujah! The Welcome Table

A Lifetime of Memories with Recipes

Maya Angelou

RANDOM HOUSE TRADE PAPERBACKS NEW YORK

2007 Random House Trade Paperback Edition

Copyright © 2004 by Maya Angelou
Photographs copyright © 2004 by Sockeye Studios

Published in the United States by Random House,
an imprint of The Random House Publishing Group, a division of
Random House, Inc., New York, and simultaneously in Canada by
Random House of Canada Limited, Toronto.

RANDOM HOUSE TRADE PAPERBACKS and colophon
are registered trademarks of Random House, Inc.

Originally published in hardcover in the United States by
Random House, an imprint of The Random House Publishing Group,
a division of Random House, Inc., in 2004.

Library of Congress Cataloging-in-Publication Data

Angelou, Maya.
Hallelujah! the welcome table / by Maya Angelou.
p.   cm.
ISBN 978-0-8129-7485-0
1. Cookery, American. 2. Angelou, Maya—Anecdotes. I. Title.
TX715.A5697 2004
641.5973—dc22   2004044902

Printed in the United States of America on acid-free paper

Random House website address: www.atrandom.com

2 4 6 8 9 7 5 3 1

Book design by Lisa Sloane

Dedication

I dedicate this book to every wannabe cook
who will dare criticism by getting into the kitchen
and stirring up some groceries.

To O, who said she wanted a big, pretty cookbook.
Well, honey, here you are.

Acknowledgments

❧ ✦ ❧

To all the great cooks whose food I have eaten and whose recipes I have read and whose stories I have heard. My thanks to Bettie Burditte, Patricia Casey, Frances Berry, Sterling Baker, and Rosa Johnson Butler, who helped me at all hours for months to compile the recipes. I am proud that frustration did not cause them to move abroad and change their names. I thank my entire family for trusting me in the kitchen. And a salute to Brian Lanker, who helped me see clearly the images of foods that were becoming fuzzy in my memory.

Here's to Brian Daigle, who drove my bus so steadily across the U.S.A. that Lydia Stuckey and I could cook everything from baked acorn squash to zucchini gratinée.

A salute to Chef Don McMillan, who, at the drop of a toque, stepped in and helped me tremendously.

Thank you all.

Maya Angelou

Contents

༄ ✦ ༄

Pie Fishing

MY GRANDMOTHER, who my brother, Bailey, and I called Momma, baked lemon meringue pie that was unimaginably good. My brother and I waited for the pie. We yearned for it, longed for it. Bailey even hinted and dropped slightly veiled suggestions about it, but none of his intimations hastened its arrival. Nor could anything he said stave off the story that came part and parcel with the pie.

Bailey would complain, "Momma, you told us that story a hundred times" or "We know what happened to the old woman" and "Momma, can we just have the pie?" (Momma always ignored his attempts to prevent her from telling the tale.) But if we wanted Momma's lemon meringue pie, we had to listen to the story:

There was an old woman who had made it very clear that she loved young men. Everyone in town knew where her interests lay so she couldn't get any local young men to come to her house. Old men had to be called to clean out her chimney or fix her roof or mend her fences. She learned to count on finding young strangers who were traveling through the area.

One Sunday morning there was a new young man in church sitting alone. Mrs. Townsend saw him and as soon as the last hymn was sung, before anyone else could reach him, she rushed over to his bench.

"Morning, I'm Hattie Townsend. What's your name?"

"George Wilson, ma'am."

She frowned a little.

"Anybody get to you?"

"No, ma'am. I don't know anyone here. Just passed by, saw the church, and stopped in." He had used the word *ma'am* out of courtesy.

She was all smiles again. "Well, then I'm inviting you, and I am a good cook, to my house for Sunday dinner. I have my own chickens and two cows, so my chickens are fresh and my butter is rich. I live in walking distance. Here is my address; come around this afternoon around three o'clock."

She patted him on the shoulder and left the church.

A few young men from the congregation rushed over.

"Mrs. Townsend invited you for dinner?"

"Yes."

"Well, I'm Bobby. Here's Taylor and this one is Raymond. We've all been to her house and she's a good cook."

The men started laughing.

"No, she's a great cook. It's just that after you eat, she pounces."

"Man, the lady can pounce."

The stranger said, "I don't mind a little pouncing."

They all laughed again. "But man, she's old. She's older than my mother."

"She's older than my grandmother."

"She's older than baseball."

The stranger said, "I'll eat dinner and after that I can take care of myself. Thanks, fellas, for warning me."

Bobby shouted, "Her lemon pie will make a rabbit hug a hound."

Taylor added, "Make a preacher lay his Bible down."

Meanwhile, Mrs. Townsend entered her house and went directly to her sewing box. She put on her glasses and took out a needle.

She walked back down the path to her house and stuck the needle in a tree.

She returned to the house and began to cook a chicken she had resting in the refrigerator. For the next hour she stirred pots and shifted pans, then she set her dining table for two. She had time to freshen up and change before her company came.

"Well, welcome, Mr. Wilson."

He was a little cooler than he had been at church.

She knew why but she also knew he hadn't eaten her cooking.

"The bathroom is here if you would like to freshen up. Dinner is not quite ready yet."

Of course everything was ready, but she wanted him to have time to breathe in the fine aromas floating in the air.

She served him chicken and dumplings. Chicken tender as mercy and dumplings light as summer clouds.

The side dishes were fried yellow summer squash and English peas.

He didn't care that he was eating as if he hadn't eaten in a month. She kept pressing him, "Eat some more, but save a place for dessert. Some people swear by my lemon meringue pie."

Between bites she thought she heard him mumble, "That's my favorite."

When he put his first bite of Mrs. Townsend's pie in his mouth, he was hers. He was ready to marry her or let her adopt him.

She sat opposite and watched as with each forkful he surrendered more.

After the second slice he would have followed her to the Sahara Desert.

She said, "Let's go out on the porch for the air."

He replied meekly, "Yes, ma'am."

Once they settled into the swing on the porch she said, "My goodness, night has fallen. It's quite dark."

"Yes, ma'am. It's dusk all right."

They swung a few times.

She asked, "What on earth is that shining down there in that tree?"

He squinted, "I can't hardly see a tree."

She said, "Yes, I see it. It's either a needle or a pin shining. Well, I do say. It's a needle."

He asked, "You can tell?"

She said, "Yes, I see the hole. I'll go get it."

He said, "Well, that proves you are not as old as they say you are. When you come back I may have some talk for you."

She stepped off the porch and went down the lane and retrieved the needle. When she came back she could hardly see the house, but she kept walking with her head up, triumph in her grasp.

She tripped in the darkness. After much fumbling she was able to stand erect. She saw that she had fallen over a cow that had lain down in the lane.

Mr. Wilson saw her fall, and he could see the cow. When she gave a little scream, he bounded off the porch to help her. Once she collected herself, he said, "Well, thank you for dinner. I have to go."

She asked, "Can't you stay for one more slice of pie?" The strength of the pie can be seen in the fact that he did stop to think about it.

She took his arm as if she wasn't going to give it back. He thought of the pie again and then the cow and the possible pouncing. He said, "No, ma'am," and snatched his arm and went away running. He escaped, but he never forgot the pie.

Each time, my grandmother laughed until tears flooded her cheeks. I think she knew Mrs. Townsend or someone very much like her.

Here is the recipe. In fact, here are the recipes for Mrs. Townsend's entire Young-Man-Catching Sunday Afternoon Dinner.

Best wishes.

Lemon Meringue Pie

SERVES 6

1 cup sugar

3 tablespoons cornstarch

1/8 teaspoon salt

1 1/2 cups hot water

1 1/2 cups crumbs from soft-type bread (no crusts)

4 large egg yolks (reserve whites for Meringue)

1 tablespoon butter

Grated rind of 1 medium lemon

Juice of 2 medium lemons

One 9-inch pie shell, baked

Meringue (recipe follows)

Preheat oven to 400°F.

In top part of double boiler, mix well sugar, cornstarch, and salt. Stir in hot water and combine until smooth. Add bread crumbs and cook over boiling water, stirring until smooth and thickened.

In small mixing bowl, beat egg yolks, and stir in a small amount of mixture. Then combine the two mixtures in boiler, and cook over low to medium heat for 2 to 3 minutes. Add butter, lemon rind, and lemon juice. Cool slightly.

Pour mixture into baked shell. Pile Meringue lightly on top, covering filling completely.

Bake for 10 minutes, or until lightly browned.

Meringue

4 large egg whites

1/8 teaspoon salt

1 teaspoon cream of tartar

4 tablespoons sugar

Beat egg whites with salt until frothy. Gradually add cream of tartar and sugar. Beat until stiff but not dry.

Chicken and Dumplings

SERVES 6 TO 8

1 whole chicken (about 4 pounds cut up)
6 chicken wings
1 large Spanish onion, chopped and sautéed but not browned
2 stalks celery, chopped
1 carrot, peeled and chopped

1 green bell pepper, chopped
Bouquet Garni (recipe follows)
Salt and freshly ground black pepper, to taste
Drop Dumplings (recipe follows)

Wash and pat dry chicken. Take flange off chicken wings.

Place cut-up chicken and wings into large, heavy pot, and add water to cover 1 inch above chicken. Add onion, celery, carrot, bell pepper, and Bouquet Garni. Season with salt and pepper. Allow mixture to simmer slowly for $1\frac{1}{2}$ hours. Let cool. Remove any foam that has gathered on top of the broth.

Bring broth to a slight boil, and drop heaping tablespoons of dumpling batter into pot. Fill top of pot with dumplings. Cover pot, and simmer for 15 minutes—dumplings will rise. Baste dumplings, and continue simmering for another 5 minutes. Remove cover and baste dumplings. Serve hot on platter.

Bouquet Garni

3 bay leaves
8 black peppercorns
Tops from two stalks of celery
1 teaspoon margarine

Cut double thickness of cheesecloth 6 inches wide. Place bay leaves, peppercorns, celery tops, and margarine in center of cheesecloth. Pull corners of cheesecloth together, and tie with kitchen twine.

Drop Dumplings

2 cups sifted all-purpose flour
¼ teaspoon salt
2 heaping teaspoons baking powder
2 tablespoons (¼ stick) butter
1 cup plus 2 tablespoons milk

Sift flour, salt, and baking powder into mixing bowl. Add butter, mixing with fingertips, then milk, until mixture is consistency of grainy cornmeal.

Fried Yellow Summer Squash

SERVES 4

5 yellow squash
1 tablespoon canola oil
1 tablespoon butter
1 cup sautéed diced onions

Salt and freshly ground black pepper, to taste
1 teaspoon fresh rosemary leaves, finely chopped

Slice squash. In large skillet, sauté squash in oil and butter. When slightly brown, add onions. Season with salt and pepper. Cook over medium heat 3 more minutes, but do not allow squash to become mushy. Sprinkle with rosemary, and keep warm until served.

Green Peas and Lettuce

SERVES 4

1 small head iceberg lettuce
2 cups fresh green peas
2 cups chicken or vegetable stock

Salt and freshly ground black pepper, to taste
½ pint heavy cream, warmed

Remove heart from lettuce, and fill with peas. Tie up lettuce head with kitchen twine to secure. Place in heavy pot with stock nearly to top of lettuce. Cover and steam until peas are tender, about 30 minutes. (Open the lettuce carefully, take one pea out, and test it.)

Remove twine and discard. Open lettuce, season with salt and pepper, and pour cream over lettuce and peas. Serve at once.

The Assurance of Caramel Cake

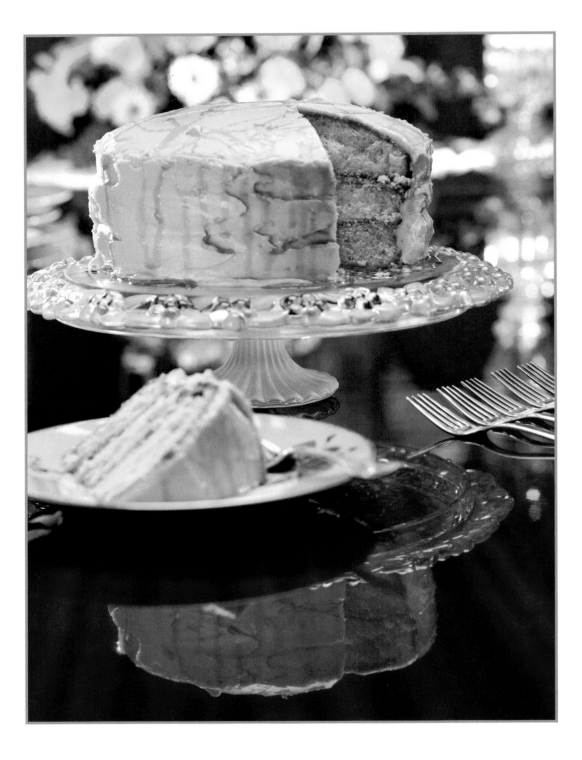

$$\approx + \approx$$

QUILTING BEES WERE EAGERLY anticipated by southern black women. They offered the only nonlabor, nonreligious occasions where women could gather and exchange all the communities' good and bad news. The women planned for weeks. Then they selected and cooked their favorite dessert dishes and brought them to the gathering. The bees were always held in the back of the store, which meant that Bailey and I could look forward to some delicious cakes and pies and, if the event took place in the summer, some luscious hand-cranked strawberry ice cream. Usually cranked by us.

Mrs. Sneed, the pastor's wife, would bring sweet potato pie, warm and a little too sweet for Momma's taste but perfect to Bailey and me. Mrs. Miller's coconut cake and Mrs. Kendrick's chocolate fudge were what Adam and Eve ate in the Garden just before the Fall. But the most divine dessert of all was Momma's Caramel Cake.

Momma would labor prayerfully over her selection, because she knew but would never admit that she and all the women were in hot competition over whose culinary masterpiece was the finest.

Momma could bake all the other women's dishes and often made them for the family, but not one of the other cooks would even dare the Caramel Cake (always to be spoken of in capital letters). Since she didn't have brown sugar, she had to make her own caramel syrup. Making her caramel cake took four to five hours, but the result was worthy of the labor. The salty sweetness of the caramel frosting along with the richness of the batter made the dessert soften and liquefy on the tongue and slip quietly down the throat almost without notice. Save that it left a memory of heaven itself in the mouth.

Of course Bailey and I were a little biased in Momma's favor, but who could have resisted the bighearted woman who was taller and bigger than most men yet who spoke in a voice a little above a whisper? Her hands were so large one could span my entire head, but they were so gentle that when she rubbed my legs and arms and face with blue-seal Vaseline every morning, I felt as if an angel had just approved of me.

I not only loved her, I liked her. So I followed her around. People began calling me her shadow.

"Hello, Sister Henderson, I see you got your shadow with you as usual." She would smile and answer, "I guess you got that right. If I go, she goes. If I stop, she stops. Yes, sir, I have me two shadows. Well, three by rights. My own and my two grandbabies."

I only saw Momma's anger become physical once. The incident alarmed me, but at the same time it assured me that I had great protection. Because of a horrible sexual violence I experienced when I was seven, I stopped talking to everyone but Bailey.

All teachers who came to Stamps to work at Lafayette County Training School had to find room and board with black families, for there were no boardinghouses where they could gain admittance.

All renting families acted as individual chambers of commerce for the newcomers. Each teacher was told of the churches and the preachers, of the hairdressers and barbers, of the white store downtown and the Wm. Johnson General Merchandise Store where they were likely to get accounts to tide them over between paychecks. The new teachers were also alerted to Mrs. Henderson's mute granddaughter and her grandson who stuttered seriously.

Summer was over and we returned to school with all the other children. I looked forward to meeting the new teacher of the fourth-, fifth-, and sixth-grade classes. I was really happy because for the first time Bailey and I were in the same classroom.

Miss Williams was small and perky. She reminded me of a young chicken pecking in the yard. Her voice was high-pitched. She separated the classes by row. Sixth-graders sat near the windows, fifth-graders were in the middle rows, and fourth-graders were near the door.

Miss Williams said she wanted each student to stand up and say his or her name and what grades they received at the end of the last semester.

She started with the sixth-graders. I looked at Bailey when he stood and said, "Bailey Johnson, Jr." At home he would make me fall out laughing when he said what he wished his whole name was: "Bailey James Jester Jonathan Johnson, Jr."

Because I didn't talk I had developed a pattern of behavior in classrooms. Whenever I was questioned, I wrote my answer on the blackboard. I had reached the blackboard in Miss Williams's room when the teacher approached me. We were nearly the same height.

She said, "Go back to your seat. Go on."

Bailey stood up over by the window.

He said, "She's going to write her name and grade on the blackboard."

Miss Williams said to me, "I've heard about you. You can talk, but you just *won't* talk."

The students, who usually teased me relentlessly, were on my side. They began explaining, "She never talks, Miss Williams, never." Bailey was nervous. He began to stutter, "My . . . Maya can't talk."

Miss Williams said, "You will talk in my classroom. Yes, you will." I didn't know what to do. Bailey and the other children were trying to persuade her to allow me to write on the blackboard. I did not resist as she took the chalk out of my hand. "I know you can talk. And I will not stand for your silliness in my classroom." I watched her as she made herself angry. "You will not be treated differently just because your people own a store."

"Speak, speak." She was fairly shouting. Her hand came up unexpectedly and she slapped me. Truly, I had not known what to do when she was winding herself up to hit me, but I knew what I had to do the second her hand landed on my cheek. I ran. I ran out of the classroom with Bailey following shouting, "Wait, My, wait." I couldn't wait. I was running to Momma. He caught up with me on the porch of the store.

Momma, hearing the noise, opened the screen door.

"What happened? Why aren't you in school? Sister, why are you crying?"

Bailey tried to answer her, but his brain moved faster than his tongue could form the words.

I took my notebook and pencil and wrote, "Miss Williams slapped me because I wouldn't talk."

"She slapped you? Slapped? Where?"

Bailey said, "Fa . . . fa . . . fa . . . face."

Momma told Bailey to go back to school. She said she and I would be coming soon.

Momma's calm voice and unhurried manner helped Bailey to settle down enough to speak.

"You want me to tell Miss Williams that you are coming?"

Momma answered, "I want you to go back to school and get your lesson." He looked at me once, saw that I had stopped crying, so he nodded and jumped off the porch and headed back up the hill.

"Sister, go to the well and put some fresh water on your face." I went around behind the store to the well.

When I returned to the porch Momma had put on one of her huge freshly washed, starched, sun-dried, and ironed aprons. In her hand she had the board that was slipped into pockets closing off the front door. We had a similar plank for the store, which we used every night to let customers know we were closed. I don't remember there being a lock for the house or the store.

Momma dropped the board into the slots, and in a second she was striding up the hill to the school.

I hurried beside, hoping to read her intentions in her face.

She looked as she always looked, serene, quiet. If she planned something unusual it did not register in her face.

She walked into the school building and turned around to me.

"Sister, show me your classroom."

I guided her to Miss Williams's room. She opened the door and Miss Williams walked up to Momma.

She asked, "Yes? May I help you?"

My grandmother asked, "Are you Miss Williams?"

Miss Williams said, "I am."

Momma asked, "Are you somebody's grandbaby?"

Miss Williams answered, "I am someone's granddaughter."

Momma said, "Well, this child here is my grandbaby." Then she slapped her. Not full force but hard enough for the sound to go around the room and to elicit gasps from the students.

"Now, Sister, nobody has the right to hit nobody in the face. So I am wrong this time, but I'm teaching a lesson." She looked at me. "Now find yourself a seat and sit down and get your lesson."

Momma left the room and it was suddenly empty and very quiet.

Miss Williams left the room for a few minutes. Not a word was spoken.

Miss Williams reentered and said, "Students, turn to lesson one on page one."

I looked at Bailey and he gave me the smallest nod. I turned to page one, lesson one.

No one spoke of the incident on the way home, and when I returned to the store Momma and Uncle Willie were sitting on the porch.

Uncle Willie said, "Sister, there's something on the kitchen table. Bring it out here please."

I went into the kitchen and on the chopping table stood the most wondrous Caramel Cake looking like paradise, oozing sweetness.

Carefully I brought it back to the porch and it was nearly worth being slapped just to hear Bailey gasp.

Uncle Willie said, "This cake can't pay you for being slapped in the face. Momma made it just to tell you how much we love you and how precious you are."

Caramel Cake

SERVES 8

8 tablespoons (1 stick) butter
1¼ cups sugar
¼ cup Caramel Syrup (recipe follows)
2 cups sifted all-purpose flour
2 teaspoons baking powder

½ teaspoon salt
1 cup milk
2 large eggs
Caramel Frosting (recipe follows)

Preheat oven to 375°F. Line two 8-inch layer cake pans with greased wax paper.

In large mixing bowl, beat butter, and add 1 cup sugar gradually until light and fluffy. Beat in syrup.

In medium mixing bowl, sift flour, baking powder, and salt together. Add sifted ingredients to creamed mixture, alternating with milk.

In separate medium mixing bowl, beat eggs about 3 minutes, until foamy. Add remaining sugar, and beat until there is a fine spongy foam. Stir into cake batter until blended.

Divide batter between cake pans. Bake for about 25 minutes. Remove pans from oven. Gently press center of cake with forefinger. Cake should spring back when finger is removed. If it doesn't, return to oven for 10 minutes. Cool in pans for 10 minutes. Turn out onto rack, and remove wax paper. Let cakes cool to room temperature before frosting.

To assemble: Center one cooled cake layer on cake plate. Cover top and sides with generous helping of frosting. Place second layer evenly on frosted layer. Repeat frosting procedure. Make certain that sides are completely frosted. Cool in refrigerator until ready to serve.

Caramel Syrup

1 cup white sugar
1 cup boiling water

Heat sugar in heavy skillet over low heat. Stir constantly until melted to a brown liquid. When it bubbles over entire surface, remove from heat. Slowly add boiling water, stirring constantly. Pour into container and cool.

Caramel Frosting

6 tablespoons (3/4 stick) butter
One 8-ounce package confectioners' sugar
4 tablespoons heavy cream
1½ teaspoons vanilla extract
Pinch of salt

Brown butter in heavy pot over medium heat—be vigilant or it will burn. Allow butter to cool. In large mixing bowl, add confectioners' sugar, cream, vanilla extract, and salt to the butter, and beat until smooth. If frosting is too stiff, add tablespoon of half-and-half or full cream to thin.

Coconut Cake

SERVES 8

2/3 cup soft butter
1 1/2 cups sugar
2 1/2 cups sifted cake flour
2 1/2 teaspoons baking powder
1/3 cup milk
4 large egg whites
1/8 teaspoon salt

1/2 teaspoon cream of tartar
4 large egg yolks
1 teaspoon vanilla extract
1 teaspoon coconut flavoring
Coconut Frosting (recipe follows)
1 cup shredded sweet coconut

Preheat oven to 350°F. Line two 9-inch layer cake pans with greased wax paper. In large mixing bowl, cream butter and sugar, beating until light and fluffy.

In medium mixing bowl, sift together flour and baking powder. Add to cream mixture, alternating with milk.

In separate medium mixing bowl, beat egg whites until foamy. Beat again for 2 minutes. Fold in salt and cream of tartar. Set aside.

In another medium mixing bowl, beat egg yolks. Add yolks to cake batter, then fold in whites, vanilla extract, and coconut flavoring.

Pour batter into layer cake pans. Bake for 30 to 35 minutes, or until cake springs back when center is pressed gently with forefinger. Cool in pans for 10 minutes; then turn out onto rack, and remove wax paper. Let cakes cool to room temperature.

To frost, place first cake layer on cake plate, and spread frosting on top. Sprinkle some coconut on top of frosting. Place second layer onto first layer, and cover entire cake with frosting. Sprinkle coconut on top of cake, and place shreds of coconut on sides of cake. Refrigerate, and serve cold.

Coconut Frosting

1 pint whipping cream
½ cup powdered sugar
1 teaspoon coconut flavoring

In medium mixing bowl, whip cream until frothy. Add sugar and coconut flavoring, and whip until it holds stiff peak.

Chocolate Fudge

MAKES ABOUT 10 PIECES

3 cups sugar
3 cups milk
2 tablespoons corn syrup
6 ounces semisweet chocolate
  pieces

3 tablespoons butter
1 teaspoon vanilla extract
1 cup chopped pecans (optional)

Butter 8 × 8-inch pan.

In large, heavy saucepan, bring sugar, milk, corn syrup, and chocolate to a boil.

Put a drop of mixture in 1 cup of ice-cold water. When the drop forms a soft ball, remove from heat. If ball does not form, continue cooking and repeat until ball forms.

Add butter and vanilla extract to hot mixture. Cool. When saucepan with chocolate mixture has cooled to a lukewarm temperature, beat mixture with spoon until it loses its gloss and becomes thick. If you want nuts, stir in pecans before mixture cools completely. Cool in pan. Cut in desired size squares.

Momma's
Grandbabies
Love
Cracklin' Cracklin'

EACH YEAR AFTER THE FIRST FROST, men and women wearing heavy clothes and carrying rifles and sawed-off shotguns stalked around inside the store buying peanut patties and candy bars.

Bailey called them the killing crew because they went around the neighborhood killing all the hogs and cows that had been selected for slaughter.

For the next two weeks, or as long as our icebox could keep the meat, we would be sure that Momma was going to cook some exquisite fresh beef and pork dishes.

She told me that she could cook a whole hog and make people love to eat it. "Everything but its hooves." She said when it came to hogs, poor people had to learn how to use everything "from the rooter [its snout] to the tooter [its tail]."

The neighborhood women would bring the hog heads and intestines to the store. They would put the heads on tables that had been set up outside between the wells and the iron pots where we washed out clothes. They would carry the intestines far beyond the outdoor toilet and empty them in a hole in the ground, dug for that purpose.

The stench was horrible, but Momma never allowed me to leave the spot and return to the store where there were the aromas of oranges and apples. "You have to know how to do this, Sister. All poor people need to know how to do some of everything, and a poor colored woman even more so. Don't turn your nose up at anything except evil."

While I bustled about helping in the stinking miasmic odor, I tried to think of the rich stew that Momma always served with crackling bread. But it was the thought of crackling bread itself that made me forget the smell of raw intestines.

Momma salted and roasted a large pan full of pork skin, which would become so crisp that it crackled. The fat rendered from the meat was stored to be used later for cooking and making soap.

She always gave a few crispy pieces of the skin to her grandbabies and to Uncle Willie, but most of the cracklings were saved for her great beef stew or until she cooked and served a large pot of collard greens. Then she'd bring out a giant pan of corn bread filled with cracklings.

The greens and stew dinner, which was always served with raw onions, pickled beets, and a jar of pepper sauce, was one of my favorite winter meals.

Although two adults and two children would share the food, Momma never reduced the size of the bread she gave us. I preferred Momma's crackling corn bread over other peoples' Sunday cake.

Crackling Corn Bread

SERVES 8

2 cups white cornmeal

¼ cup sifted all-purpose flour

1 tablespoon sugar

½ teaspoon salt

4 teaspoons baking powder

1½ cups plus 2 tablespoons milk

2 large eggs, beaten well

2 tablespoons (¼ stick) butter, melted

½ pound crisp cracklings,* broken into ½-inch pieces

Preheat oven to 350°F. Grease an 8 × 8 × 2-inch pan.

Mix dry ingredients; stir in milk and eggs. Pour in butter, and add cracklings. Pour mixture into pan and bake for 1 hour, or until brown and firm.

*Cracklings are called *chicharones* in Spanish and can be found in Latino grocery stores.

Momma's Rich Beef Stew

SERVES 8

3 pounds chuck, cut into bite-size
  pieces

Salt and freshly ground black pepper, to taste

½ cup all-purpose flour

⅓ cup vegetable oil

3 cups water

1 teaspoon salt

½ teaspoon freshly ground
  black pepper

3 bay leaves

1 teaspoon fresh chopped parsley

1 onion, cut into large pieces

2 turnips, peeled and cut into large
  pieces

1 rutabaga, peeled and cut into
  large pieces

2 white potatoes, peeled and cut
  into large pieces

1 parsnip, peeled and cut into large
  pieces

3 carrots, peeled and cut into large
  pieces

1 green bell pepper, cut into large
  pieces

Season beef with salt and pepper, then dredge in flour. Pour oil in large pot over medium heat. Add beef, and brown all sides in oil. Add water, salt and pepper, bay leaves, and parsley, and cook simmering for 1 hour.

Add vegetables. Check seasoning, and bring vegetables and meat back to boil. Cover stew, and cook on medium. When meat and vegetables are tender, take stew off heat and let rest for 15 to 20 minutes.

Serve with good Italian bread or Crackling Corn Bread (p. 27).

Collard Greens

2 smoked turkey wings

3 bunches tender collards (the greens are better if they are picked after the first frost)

1 sweet onion, chopped

2 hot red peppers

Salt and freshly ground black pepper, to taste

1 tablespoon sugar

In large pot, boil turkey wings in water to cover for 1 hour.

Pick and wash greens, and discard large stems. Chop leaves coarsely.

Add all ingredients to pot. Simmer for 1½ hours, adding water if needed. When greens are done, they can be served with Crackling Corn Bread (p. 27).

Potato Salad Towers Over Difficulties

WE WERE MEMBERS of the CME Church and for years I thought the initials stood for Colored Methodist Episcopal Church. Then I was told that the letters described the Christian Methodist Episcopal Church. Later I discovered I had been right the first time. But in Arkansas, and possibly in all the states, there were Presiding Elders, who were the crème de la crème, and they wouldn't have it otherwise.

The pompous Presiding Elder who served our region would arrive in town on horseback or, on the rare occasion, in a car, always with someone else driving. He would stay with other parishioners, but at every three-month visit he told Bailey and me that until our arrival he was always put up by Mother Henderson and Superintendent Johnson. (Uncle Willie was superintendent of the Sunday school.) We never knew what to say. Did he think we should get back on the train and return to parents who obviously had no place for us in their lives?

To say Bailey and I hated the Presiding Elder could not describe our bitter loathing for the puffed-up man who had no sensitivity to two wayfaring motherless and fatherless children.

He didn't sleep at Momma's house, but he took every meal there, and *took* is the correct word. Because of him, Bailey and I spent the most embarrassing hour of our lives, and to add insult to injury we became very sick.

Piss Ant, as Bailey called him, came round as usual after Sunday services. I brought him a face basin with water from the well so he could wash, but he hardly dipped his hand in the water, nor did he say thank you. I turned to go in the kitchen to help Momma, but I saw Bailey had seen Piss Ant's behavior.

Momma sent me to the garden to pick and wash lettuce. She had made her delicious potato salad. She chipped off a corner from a block of ice and pulverized it with a hammer. She put the lettuce in a pretty dish and laid crushed ice between the leaves.

When Momma called everyone in for Sunday dinner, the table was powerful with her delectables spread from end to end. There was the most golden-brown fried chicken, string beans with little potatoes, dark green turnip leaves with snow-white turnips, pickled peaches, and a platter of her buttermilk biscuits called cat heads because of their size. But the star of that show was the potato salad. Momma had mixed all the ingredients, then mounded the salad high above the top of the bowl. She had hard-boiled four double-yolk eggs and cut them in half and pushed them down into the potato mixture; then she placed crisp cucumber circles around the inside edges of the bowl.

Each person was supposed to pick up the fork in the lettuce bowl and take one leaf up, let it drip in the bowl, then place it on the salad plate just to the left of the dinner plate. Then a spoon of potato salad would be placed on the lettuce leaf. That was how we did it, how *everybody* did it except for the Presiding Elder. He glanced at the chicken and immediately took the three largest pieces. Then he used his own fork to serve himself potato salad.

Bailey cleared his throat and asked, "Would you like some lettuce?" Piss Ant was so used to ignoring children that he didn't even look at Bailey. He picked up the potato salad and fished out three of the halves of double-yolk eggs and put them on his plate beside the chicken. Then he completed filling his plate with the salad.

His mouth was so stuffed we could hardly understand him. "Save me some greens, sure have a soft spot for greens."

Bailey's face was a mask of angry disgust, and I knew he was going to do something. Just what, I wasn't sure. When Momma looked at her grandson, she also had a premonition.

Bailey hesitated only a second. Using the lettuce fork, he speared every leaf in the bowl, held it up to drip, and then put the whole thing on his plate.

Momma reared back and pursed her lips. She didn't speak. She turned and started to prepare Uncle Willie's plate. Bailey looked at me. I wanted to laugh but didn't dare, but I was pleased that he had the nerve to get that Presiding Elder good. I did give Bailey a little nod and he nodded back. Then he took the whole stack of lettuce and started to put it back into its receptacle. Momma said, "No, sir, little master, you will eat every bit of that lettuce before you get up from this table."

Momma didn't like the Presiding Elder either, but she was a stickler for the way to do things and the ways they shouldn't be done.

Bailey sat back in his chair and surveyed the situation. Then he pulled up to the table, and taking one forefinger he flicked one of the leaves into his lap, slid it over to me, and got one more himself. He showed me how to roll the leaf like a cigarette and munch it.

We ate the entire bowl of lettuce—and only the lettuce—for Sunday dinner. After the Presiding Elder left, Momma and Uncle Willie sat on the porch laughing. They would not admit to us that they had been laughing at Bailey, but Momma called us outside.

"Now, young missy and young master, I know your stomachs are upset. I've seen how many times you went out to the little outhouse. You didn't have to make yourselves sick. I have told you never be concerned at how much others may have. I always keep something in the kitchen for Grandma and the children."

That evening she gave us chicken from the oven and potato salad from the icebox.

Cold Potato Salad

SERVES 6 TO 8

6 cups peeled, diced, cooked potatoes

1 medium onion, finely chopped

1 cup finely diced celery

1 cup chopped dill pickles

1 cup sweet relish, drained

8 large hard-boiled eggs, 4 chopped, 4 whole

Salt and freshly ground black pepper, to taste

1½ cups mayonnaise

Fresh parsley, chopped

Combine potatoes, onion, celery, pickles, relish, and chopped eggs. Season with salt and pepper, and add mayonnaise. Chill for several hours. Just before serving, halve the remaining 4 eggs, and place on salad as decoration. Dust salad with parsley, and serve at once.

Fried Chicken

One 2-pound chicken
1 cup lemon juice
1 teaspoon salt
½ teaspoon freshly ground
 black pepper

1 cup all-purpose flour
2 cups Crisco oil

Wash and pat dry chicken. Cut into pieces, place in a container, and add lemon juice. Put in refrigerator, covered, for 1 hour. Rinse, dry, and season with salt and pepper. Dredge chicken in flour.

In a large pot, heat oil. Add chicken pieces, and cover. Fry on high heat until brown on both sides.

Reduce heat to low-medium, cover, and cook for 30 minutes.

Remove from heat, and drain on paper towels. Serve hot.

Snow-White Turnips

SERVES 4

8 small turnips, peeled
6 whole cloves
⅛ teaspoon salt

1 tablespoon sugar
2 tablespoons (¼ stick) butter

Place turnips, cloves, and salt in a heavy saucepan. Cover with water. Boil until turnips are tender, about 20 to 30 minutes. Remove from stove, drain, and discard cloves. Add sugar, and stir until sugar dissolves. Add butter, and stir to melt. Serve at once.

Mustard and Turnip Greens with Smoked Turkey Wings

2 smoked turkey wings

3 pounds mustard greens

1 pound young, tender turnip
  greens

½ teaspoon sugar

Salt, to taste

Place turkey wings in large pot, and cover with water. Boil until nearly tender, about 45 minutes to an hour.

Wash and drain greens. Put in pot with cooked meat. Add sugar and season with salt. Add enough water to cover, and simmer until tender.

Drain and reserve liquid, which is called pot liquor and will be very good the next day with corn bread. Remove meat from bones, chop, and add to greens. Serve at once.

Pickled Peaches

SERVES 6

6 medium nearly ripe peaches,
   peeled and pitted
¾ cup sugar
⅛ teaspoon salt

½ cup cider vinegar
1 cup orange juice
1 tablespoon whole cloves
2 cinnamon sticks

Put peaches in large pot, add sugar, salt, vinegar, juice, cloves, and cinnamon sticks, and cover with water. Boil for 30 minutes. Take off stove, and let cool. Put in refrigerator in its own liquid. Discard cinnamon and cloves. Serve cold.

Buttermilk Biscuits

4 cups all-purpose flour
½ teaspoon salt
6 teaspoons baking powder
1 teaspoon baking soda

1 cup lard
2 cups buttermilk
All-purpose flour

Preheat oven to 375°F.

Sift flour with salt, baking powder, and baking soda. Cut in lard until mixture resembles coarse cornmeal. Add buttermilk, and stir until dough leaves side of bowl.

Turn dough out onto a lightly floured board, and knead until smooth. Roll out to ½-inch thickness, and cut into 2-inch rounds. If there is no biscuit cutter at hand, use a water glass. (Turn glass upside down, dust rim in flour, and cut biscuits.)

Bake on ungreased cookie sheet for 20 to 25 minutes, or until biscuits are golden brown.

Liver to Grow On

I N STAMPS, WOMEN PRESERVED everything that would submit to the process. After the first frost, when men killed the hogs and cows selected for slaughter, Momma, with the aid of the missionary ladies of the Christian Methodist Episcopal Church, would prepare the meat for sausage. I enjoyed watching them. They would grind the raw pork, then squeeze their arms elbow deep in the ground meat, mixing it with gray nose-opening sage, pepper and salt, and red pepper. They often fried tasty little samples for all obedient children who brought wood for the slick black stove. The men chopped off the larger pieces of pork and laid them in the smokehouse to begin the curing process. They opened the knuckle of the hams with their deadly-looking knives, took out a certain round, harmless-looking bone ("It could make the meat too bad"), and rubbed coarse brown salt that looked like fine gravel into the flesh, and watched as the blood popped to the surface.

Throughout the year, until the next frost, we took our meals from the smokehouse, the chicken coop, the shelves of canned goods, and the little garden that lay cousin-close to the store. There were choices on the shelves that could set a hungry child's mouth to watering. Green beans, snapped always the right length; collards; cabbage; juicy, sweet red tomato preserves that came into their own on steaming buttered biscuits; and sausage, beets, berries, and every fruit grown in Arkansas.

But at least twice yearly Momma would feel that her grandbabies needed fresh meat in their diets. We were then given money—pennies, nickels, and dimes entrusted to Bailey—and sent to the butcher to buy liver. The butcher shop was in the white part of town.

Crossing our area of Stamps, which in childhood's narrow measure seemed a whole world, obliged us by custom to stop and speak to every black person we met. Bailey also felt constrained to spend a few minutes playing with each friend. There I felt a special joy in going through the black area with time on our hands and money in our pockets. (Bailey's pockets were as good as my own.) But the pleasure fled when we reached the white part of town. Suddenly we were explorers walking without weapons into man-eating animals' territory.

We never turned to look at the houses we passed, nor did we really speak to each other once we were in enemy territory. We solemnly moved forward to our goal.

At the butcher shop we were lucky if no one came in. All whites were served before us, even if the butcher was half into our order. He would put our meat on the side and serve the white customer. In fact, a black maid or cook would be served before us, because her order was intended for white people. Bailey and I would stand around, never looking at each other, until there were no more calls on the butcher's time. Then we would get the liver Momma wanted to cook for our health and make our way back across the white zone I considered the frozen tundra, again wending through the black residential area where every house seemed to sing "Welcome" and on to the store and Momma and the hot skillet. The aromas of fried bacon and onions told us that all of them—the skillet, the stove, and Momma—had been waiting for the liver.

The liver dinner marked the only time when my grandmother and Uncle Willie let us have the best parts of the meat. They both chose small portions.

Momma said, "You are all growing. Liver is good for your bones and your blood. So go on, eat it. You'll be better for it."

Twenty years had to pass before I could honestly say I loved liver well prepared. Bailey never came to accept it. But we chewed it and swallowed it, and it helped us to grow and maybe it did make us better human beings.

Liver and Onions

1 pound bacon

5 medium onions, sliced

1 pound thinly sliced beef liver

2 tablespoons all-purpose flour

1 teaspoon salt

½ teaspoon freshly ground black pepper

2 tablespoons vegetable oil

¾ cup water

Fry bacon in large skillet on medium heat, and remove from heat. Do not discard grease. Place bacon on paper towels to drain.

Using same skillet, cook onions in bacon fat until golden brown. Remove from heat, and place on paper towels to drain.

Mix together flour, salt, and pepper, and dust liver with mixture. Heat oil in a large skillet, and fry lightly until browned on both sides. Remove liver and pour ¾ cup water into hot skillet. Scrape bottom of skillet. Season with salt and pepper if desired. Pour hot broth over liver. Serve at once with onions and crisp bacon.

Recipes
from
Another
Country

MY GRANDMOTHER DID NOT SUBSCRIBE to the Lafayette County *Demo-crat* newspaper, saying, "It is written by white folks, about white folks, for white folks."

We received *The Chicago Defender* and *The Pittsburgh Courier* newspapers although they were published in the far-away northern cities and arrived by mail at least a week late.

However, once a month, the *Democrat* published a women's page. The page held notices of weddings, engagements, and a few recipes that were sent in by readers with their names attached. Momma knew all the names and the maids who worked for them.

On the morning when the women's page was published, as the maids passed the store on their way to work, Momma would choose one.

"Sister Bishop, I hope you'll be able to bring me that page this evening."

The woman would smile, proud to have been chosen. "Yes, ma'am, Sister Henderson. Be glad to."

The other women in the group would compliment the chosen one amid much laughter. That evening the maid would bring a folded newspaper page, and Momma would take a Babe Ruth from the icebox or a peanut patty from the candy counter.

"You know I'm not trying to pay you. Just saying thank you."

Momma would sit down and gingerly put on her glasses. Immediately she would start tsking. (In the African American community, that gesture is called sucking your teeth.)

I would wait for her comments.

"Uh-huh-huh, these white folks. What will they stop at next?" She wagged her head. "They're making gravy with beer. You know what beer is, Sister?"

I would write, "Yes, ma'am. It's white lightning."

"That's right, uh-huh. You ready to start?"

We sat together under the lamplight so many nights copying recipes that I can pull a perfect image of me and Momma bending over the kitchen table, scrutinizing the news page.

Momma said, "Now, here is one for you. It's called wilted lettuce. Don't that beat all? I have to buy ice to make my lettuce crisp up, and here is a recipe for wilted lettuce.

"This cook didn't know all she had to do to make this dish is wash the lettuce and leave it on the counter. It will wilt for you in thirty minutes."

Then she thought again. "We have some nice lettuce in the garden. I'm going to make this dish tomorrow."

The next day we sat down to Momma's version of wilted lettuce, and much to her surprise we all enjoyed it. I ate the silken side dish and wondered about the white woman who lived in the white part of town about a mile from the black area, which was still called the Quarters.

Would she think that a black grandmother was feeding her grandchildren the same dish she was offering to her privileged family?

Would she resent the grandmother or just shrug her shoulders and say, "Let them help themselves"?

I'd like to think she shrugged.

Wilted Lettuce

6 slices of bacon

6–8 green onions (white and green parts), sliced

1 tablespoon sugar

¼ teaspoon salt

⅓ cup vinegar

1 cup water

¼ teaspoon freshly ground black pepper

2 heads Boston or Bibb lettuce, leaves washed and separated

Cut bacon into small pieces, and fry in medium skillet until crisp. Remove from heat, and drain on paper towels. Add green onions, sugar, salt, vinegar, water, and pepper to bacon fat in skillet. Cook over medium heat for 5 minutes.

Put lettuce into salad bowl. Pour onion mixture over lettuce, and stir. Top with crisp bacon, and serve immediately.

❦

Independence
Forever

IN 1903, MOMMA had been married five years and had two sons. One bright morning, her husband told her that he was leaving. He explained that he had received a call—the Call—to preach. To study and prepare for that awesome responsibility, he had to travel to Ada, Oklahoma, where an elderly preacher he had met at a conference would school him. Years later Annie Henderson found that the old Oklahoma preacher had had a beautiful and marriageable daughter and that my grandfather quickly began to court her. When it was legally possible, he married the daughter and never returned to Arkansas.

My grandmother was left with a two-room shack, a lively four-year-old who would later become my father, and a two-year-old boy who was crippled.

For most of her life Annie Henderson blamed herself for Uncle Willie's condition. As a one-year-old he had crawled out of the house and had fallen off the porch to the ground.

No amount of doctors were able to convince my grandmother that Uncle Willie's paralysis was caused by a neurological malady rather than by what she thought of as her neglect.

She also laid my grandfather's departure to his displeasure at having a crippled son. So again, she was to blame.

She looked around at her situation. She was a colored woman in the South at the beginning of the twentieth century. She had herself and her sons to feed, house, and clothe. She would not work as a maid, for that would mean leaving her tots, especially her crippled one, in someone else's care. She decided to make use of the two largest employers in Stamps. They were the cotton gin, and three miles away, the lumber mill. She devised a plan that would let her make money and at the same time mostly stay at home with her "darlings."

At night she would cook and then grind and season ham and chicken and also make a batter for her cakes. Sunrise found her kneading the dough and placing the meat in the center of each pastry. Midmorning she walked from her house, leaving a young girl to watch her boys for three hours.

Carrying her fresh raw pies, her coal pot, lard, and a fold-up chair, she would arrive at the factory. She placed herself and supplies on the ground adjacent to the door the black workers used. She would begin frying pies a half hour before noon.

She told me many times that nothing sounds as loud as the dinner bell and nothing smells as good as fresh fried pies. She had a bell that she rang seconds after the noon siren sounded.

She sold the pies hot at the cotton gin for five cents. She would wrap any leftovers in a fresh tea towel, and leaving her cooking utensils under the care of a child hired for that purpose, she would run three miles to the lumber mill and offer the tepid pies for three cents. But believing in fair play and being a good businesswoman, the establishment that received lukewarm pies on one day would be her first stop the next noon. Her customers appreciated her cooking, her promptness, and her sense of fairness.

After a few years of serving the pies in both unbreathable summer heat and bone-shaking winter cold, Momma built a little hut equidistant between the two hives of commercial activity. Then at noontime the hungry workers would run to her to get their steaming chicken and cured ham pies.

Momma told me, "Sister, the world might try to put you on a road that you don't like. First stop and look behind you. If nothing back there makes you want to return, then look ahead. If nothing ahead beckons you enough to keep you going, then you have to step off that road and cut yourself a brand-new path."

The hut became a store in which I grew up. It remained in use for over sixty years.

Fried Meat Pies

1 recipe Buttermilk Biscuits dough
  (p. 41)
2 cups cooked shredded pork or
  chicken
Salt and freshly ground black
  pepper, to taste

Pinch of cinnamon
1/4 teaspoon red pepper flakes
1 cup caramelized onions (about 3
  medium onions)
5 tablespoons vegetable oil

Roll out dough to 1/4-inch thickness. Cut out circles, using salad plate. Season meat with salt and pepper, and add cinnamon and red pepper flakes. Place 2 tablespoons of meat off-center on dough circle. Put 1/2 teaspoon caramelized onions on meat. Fold dough to make a half-moon. Seal pie by pressing edges with fork tines. Refrigerate for 1 hour. Fry in 3 tablespoons oil on both sides on medium heat until golden brown.

To caramelize onions: Put 2 tablespoons of oil in frying pan, and add thinly sliced onions. Cook over medium-high heat, stirring constantly. When onions begin to brown, turn heat down. Continue to stir. Onions will become dark golden brown. Remove from heat.

❧ ✦ ❧

Early Lessons
from a
Kitchen Stool

My
Big Brother's
Savings Account

My ten-year-old son had a huge appetite and I had a very slim wallet. We lived in a small two-room apartment in a San Francisco Victorian. Our building provided cooking privileges for all tenants in a large kitchen down the hall.

I adored my brother, Bailey, and he was coming for dinner. I wanted to delight him by creating a new recipe. I would at the same time satisfy my always-hungry son.

Bailey was two years older than I and seven inches shorter, but he made it very clear all my life that he was my big brother. He was a good cook, and occasionally brilliance would overtake him at the stove and his culinary efforts would bedazzle. Our mother, who was the best and most adventurous cook in our family, encouraged us to be daring in creating recipes and bold in competing with each other.

I couldn't afford the ham Bailey loved, so I bought three smoked pork chops instead, which I planned to sauté and then bake with cooked apples, pineapples, and brown sugar, and I would serve braised cabbage with ginger as a side dish. I had just placed the pork chops in the skillet over a medium fire when the doorbell rang.

Bailey entered carrying a shopping bag. He was early and full of laughter. He said, "I brought dinner and I'm going to cook it." I said, "Well, I was going to cook pork chops and cabbage." He laughed and said, "Look in the shopping bag."

I emptied the contents onto the counter. There were three fresh pork chops, a head of cabbage, a green bell pepper, and a pound of bacon. He said, "I presume you have milk and another skillet."

I said, "Yes."

He said, "Let's cook together. I'm going to make a dish that will feed you and Guy for a week." He used half of the stove and I the other, and we shared a bottle of Mateus rosé wine for the next hour. He asked me to cook the rice since I make no-fail rice, and he expected that we would finish our dishes at the same time.

My son's eyes enlarged when he looked at the food-loaded table. My pork chops with the apple and pineapple were on one platter. Bailey's pork chops with bacon and a cream sauce were on the other. The molded rice towered in the middle of the table. I had served gingered cabbage and Bailey had made cabbage with celery and water chestnuts.

As he opened the door to leave, Bailey said, "Split one pork chop down to the bone, serve it with gravy, a piece of bacon, and rice—that would be one dinner. The next night serve just bacon and gravy and rice with a salad. There's another meal. Wait a couple of days and use another half pork chop, serve with spinach, rice, and gravy, or make some great biscuits, and that will be yet another dinner. Make a green salad in between. Do that and you'll be okay for a week."

As he started down the steps, he said, "If I had a million dollars, you would never have to wonder how you were going to feed my nephew. Since I don't have even a thousand dollars, a big brother can teach his little sister how she can save pennies and still keep her little crumb crusher from starving."

I shouted, "He is not a crumb crusher."

Bailey laughed and started around the building. I was yelling at the night air.

Bailey's Smothered Pork Chops

SERVES 6

6 thick slices bacon

1 large Spanish onion, sliced

6 end loin pork chops

Salt and freshly ground black
pepper, to taste

1 cup all-purpose flour

2 tablespoons vegetable oil,
if needed

1 cup hot water

1 cup milk

Fry bacon in large skillet on medium heat, and remove to paper towels to drain.

Sauté onion in same skillet with bacon fat, and remove to paper towels to drain.

Season pork chops with salt and pepper, and dredge in flour. Fry on medium heat in the same skillet with bacon fat until light brown, and remove to warm plate.

Put remaining flour into skillet (add oil if necessary). Brown flour lightly. Add hot water immediately, and then milk. Stir vigorously. Season as desired with more salt and pepper.

Put pork chops, bacon, and onion into gravy, and reduce heat to simmer. Cover skillet, and simmer for 20 minutes.

Check gravy for seasoning. Adjust as needed while food is still hot.

Smoked Pork Chops

SERVES 3 TO 5

1 tablespoon vegetable oil
3 large smoked pork chops
1 quart hot water
1 tablespoon butter
2 Granny Smith apples, peeled,
  cored, and diced

One 8-ounce can crushed
  pineapple, drained
1 tablespoon brown sugar
1/8 teaspoon cinnamon
1/8 teaspoon nutmeg
1/8 cup water

Preheat oven to 350°F.

Place oil and chops in large, deep skillet, and pour hot water over chops. Simmer for 20 minutes, turning chops twice while water is simmering. Take skillet off heat. Remove chops from water, and discard water. Pat chops dry.

Place butter in small pan, and add apples. Sauté apples until they are tender. Add pineapple, brown sugar, cinnamon, and nutmeg, and cook until all liquid has disappeared.

Put chops in an accommodating baking dish. Cover with apple-pineapple mixture. Pour water into bottom of dish, and cover. Bake for 30 minutes. Remove cover and continue baking for 20 minutes.

Braised Cabbage with Ginger

SERVES 4

1 medium to large head of cabbage

2 tablespoons (¼ stick) butter

¼ cup chopped onion

2 tablespoons peeled, grated fresh ginger

1 large green bell pepper, chopped

1 cup chicken bouillon

Salt and freshly ground black pepper, to taste

Quarter cabbage, remove stalk, and cover with boiling water. Let sit for 10 minutes. Drain cabbage, and pat dry in a towel. Remove to chopping board, and cut into bite-size pieces.

Melt butter over moderate heat and add cabbage, onion, ginger, bell pepper, and bouillon. Sauté until tender but not brown. Cover and cook over medium heat an added 20 minutes. Season with salt and pepper. Serve at once.

Cabbage with Celery and Water Chestnuts

SERVES 4 TO 6

1 large onion, sliced

1 green bell pepper, cut into large
   pieces

3 stalks of celery, chopped

2 tablespoons vegetable oil

1 head cabbage, cut into large
   bite-size pieces

1 cup water

One 8-ounce can water chestnut
   slices, drained

Salt and freshly ground black
   pepper, to taste

Sauté onion, bell pepper, and celery in oil until translucent but not brown. Add cabbage and water, cover, and simmer for 25 to 30 minutes. Add water chestnut slices to cabbage. Season with salt and pepper. Cook 10 more minutes, and serve.

❦ ✦ ❧

Short Ribs
à la
the Big Easy

⧼⧽ ✦ ⧼⧽

C AN YOU COOK CREOLE?"
           I looked at the woman and gave her a lie as soft as melting butter. "Yes, of course. That's all I know how to cook."

The Creole Café had a cardboard sign in the window that announced, COOK WANTED. SEVENTY-FIVE DOLLARS A WEEK. As soon as I saw it I knew I could cook Creole, whatever that was.

Desperation to find help must have blinded the proprietress to my age, or perhaps it was the fact that I was six feet and had an attitude that belied my seventeen years. She didn't question me about recipes and menus, but her long brown face did trail down in wrinkles, and doubt hung on the edges of her questions.

"Can you start on Monday?"

"I'll be glad to."

"You know it's six days a week. We're closed on Sunday."

"That's fine with me. I like to go to church on Sunday." It's awful to think that the devil gave me that lie, but it came unexpectedly and worked like dollar bills. Suspicion and doubt fled from her face, and she smiled. Her teeth were all the same size, a small white picket fence semicircled in her mouth.

"Well, I know we're going to get along. You're a good Christian. I like that. Yes, ma'am, I sure do."

My need for a job stiffed my telling (confessing to) her that I mean to be a Christian but that I blow it every day. Instead, I asked her, "What time on Monday? Bless the Lord!"

"You get here at five."

Five in the morning. Those mean streets menaced by thugs who had not yet

| 77 |

gone to sleep, pillowing on someone else's dreams. Five! Just when the streetcars began to rattle, their lighted insides looking like exclusive houses in the fog. Five!

"All right, I'll be here at five, Monday morning."

"You'll cook the dinners and put them on the steam table. You don't have to do short orders. I do that."

Mrs. Dupree was a short, plump woman of about fifty. Her hair was naturally straight and heavy. Probably Cajun, Indian, African, and white, and, naturally, Negro.

"And what's your name?"

"Rita." Marguerite was too solemn and Maya too fancy. Rita sounded like dark, flashing eyes, hot peppers, and Creole evenings with strummed guitars. "Rita Johnson."

"That's a right nice name." Then, as some people do to show their sense of familiarity, she immediately narrowed the name down. "I'll call you Reet. Okay?"

Okay, of course. I had a job. Seventy-five dollars a week. So I was Reet. Reet, poteet, and gone. All Reet. Now all I had to do was learn to cook. I asked old Papa Ford to teach me.

He had been a grown man when the twentieth century was born and left a large family of brothers and sisters in Terre Haute, Indiana (always called the East Coast), to find what the world had in store for a "good-looking colored boy with no education in his head, but a pile of larceny in his heart." He traveled with circuses "shoveling elephant shit." He shot dice in freight trains and played poker in back rooms and shanties all over the northern states. He worked as a chef on Pullman dining cars and was a fry cook in the Merchant Marine Corps.

By 1943, when I first saw him at my mother's house in San Francisco, his good looks were as delicate as an old man's memory, and disappointment rode his face bareback. His hands had gone. His gambler's fingers had thickened. During the Depression he worked at the only straight job he knew, which was carpentering. That had further toughened his "moneymakers." Mother rescued him from a job as a sweeper in a pinochle parlor and brought him home to look after the house and five roomers who rented from us.

He sorted and counted the linen when the laundry truck picked it up and returned it, then grudgingly handed out fresh sheets to the roomers. He cooked massive and delicious dinners when Mother was busy, and he sat in the tall-ceiling kitchen drinking coffee by the potfuls.

Papa Ford loved my mother (as did nearly everyone) with a childlike devotion. He went so far as to control his profanity when she was around, knowing she couldn't abide cursing unless she was doing the cursing.

When I told him I had a job as a cook and needed his help, he said, "Why the sheeit do you want to work in a goddamn kitchen washing dishes?"

"Papa, the job pays seventy-five dollars a week and I'll be cooking, not washing dishes."

"Colored women been cooking so long, thought you'd be tired of it by now."

"If you'll just tell me how to cook a few dishes . . ."

"High school and all that education. How come you don't get a goddamn job where you can go to work looking like something?"

I tried another tack. "I probably couldn't learn to cook Creole food anyway. It's too complicated."

"Sheeit. Ain't nothing but onions, celery, green peppers, garlic, and tomatoes. Put that in everything and you got Creole food. I already told you how to cook rice."

"Yes." I could cook rice till each grain stood separately.

"That's all, then. Them geechees can't live without swamp seed." He crackled at his joke, then recalled with a frown, "Still don't like you working as a goddamn cook. Get married. Then you don't have to cook for nobody but your own family. Sheeit. Yeah, don't forget, put red chili pepper in everything. They'll be expecting it."

The Creole Café steamed with onion vapor, garlic mists, tomato fogs, and green pepper sprays. I put the Creole flavors into Vivian Baxter's recipe for short ribs of beef, and Salisbury steak was just hamburger with a Creole sauce.

Mrs. Dupree chose the daily menu and left a note on the steam table informing me of her gastronomic decisions. But I, Rita, the chef, decided how much garlic and how many bay leaves would flavor the steamed Shreveport tripe. For over a month I was embroiled in the mysteries of the kitchen with the expectancy of an alchemist about to discover the secret properties of gold.

Only after the mystery had worn down to a layer of commonness did I begin to notice the customers. They consisted largely of light-skinned, slick-haired Creoles from Louisiana, who spoke French patois only a little less complicated than the contents of my pots and equally spicy. I thought it fitting and not at all unusual that they enjoyed my cooking. I was following Papa Ford's instructions loosely and adding artistic touches of my own. Mrs. Dupree said I was building up her business.

Our customers never just ate, paid, and left. They sat for hours on the long backless stools and exchanged gossip or shared the patient philosophy of the black South.

Near the steam counter, the soft sounds of black talk, the sharp reports of laughter, and the shuffling feet on tiled floors mixed themselves in odorous vapors. I was content. My cooking was appreciated. I had pockets full of money and my son was well looked after. I may not have been happy. I was content.

Braised Short Ribs
of Beef

SERVES 8

5 pounds beef short ribs, cut into
 3-inch pieces

Salt and freshly ground black
 pepper, to taste

½ teaspoon meat tenderizer

All-purpose flour

2 tablespoons vegetable oil

3 cups meat stock or water

5 medium carrots, peeled and cut
 into 1½-inch pieces

One 28-ounce can tomatoes

One 6-ounce can tomato paste

2 large onions, diced

3 stalks celery, chopped

3 cloves garlic, diced

2 green bell peppers, cut into large
 pieces

2 bay leaves

1 cup good cabernet sauvignon

1 tablespoon chopped fresh parsley

Preheat oven to 350°F.

Season meat with salt and pepper, sprinkle with meat tenderizer, and dust with flour. (I sprinkle meat tenderizer on all meat, since I expect it to be tough.) Brown on all sides in oil in Dutch oven. Add stock; cover and bake in the oven for 1 hour.

Remove from oven and add carrots, tomatoes, tomato paste, onions, celery, garlic, bell peppers, bay leaves, and wine. Return to oven, and cook 1½ hours. Meat should be very tender. Remove bay leaves, and adjust seasoning as needed.

On large serving dish, arrange vegetables around meat, and sprinkle with parsley.

Mother's
Long View

INDEPENDENCE IS A HEADY DRAFT, and if you drink it in your youth it can have the same effect on the brain as young wine. It does not matter that its taste is not very appealing; it is addictive and with each drink the consumer wants more.

When I was twenty and living in San Francisco, I had a three-year-old son, two jobs, and two rented rooms with cooking privileges down the hall. My landlady, Mrs. Jefferson, was kind and grandmotherly. She was a ready babysitter and insisted on providing dinner for her tenants. Her ways were so tender and her personality so sweet that no one was mean enough to discourage her disastrous culinary exploits. Spaghetti at her table, which was offered at least three times a week, was a mysterious red, white, and brown concoction. We would occasionally encounter an unidentifiable piece of meat floating on the plate.

There was no money in my budget to afford restaurant food, so my son and I were often loyal, if unhappy, diners at Chez Jefferson.

My mother had moved from Post Street into a fourteen-room Victorian house on Fulton Street, which she had filled with gothic, heavily carved furniture. The upholstery on the sofa and occasional chairs was red-wine-colored mohair. Oriental rugs were placed throughout the house. She had a live-in employee who was a fill-in cook for her and cleaned the house.

Mother picked up Guy two or three times a week and took him to her house where she fed him peaches and cream and hot dogs, but I only went to her house when she was expecting me.

My mother understood and encouraged my self-reliance. We had a standing appointment, which I looked forward to eagerly. Once a month, she would cook one of my favorite dishes and I would go to her house for lunch. One important date that stands out in my mind I call Vivian's Red Rice Day.

When I arrived at the Fulton Street house my mother was dressed beautifully, her makeup was perfect, and she wore good jewelry.

After we embraced, I washed my hands and we walked through her formal dark dining room and into the large bright kitchen.

Much of lunch was already on the table. Vivian Baxter cooked wonderful meals and was very serious about how to present them.

On that long-ago Red Rice Day, my mother had placed on the table a dry, crispy, roasted capon, no dressing or gravy, and a simple lettuce salad, no tomatoes or cucumbers. A widemouthed bowl covered with a platter sat next to her plate.

She blessed the table with a fervent but brief prayer and put her left hand on the platter and her right on the bowl and turned the dishes over. She gently loosened the bowl from its contents and revealed a tall mound of glistening red rice (my favorite food in all the world) decorated with finely minced parsley and the green tops of scallions.

The chicken and salad do not feature so prominently on my taste buds' memory, but each grain of red rice is emblazoned on the surface of my tongue forever.

Gluttonous and *greedy* negatively describe the hearty eater offered the seduction of her favorite food.

Two large portions of rice sated my appetite, but the deliciousness of the dish made me long for a larger stomach so that I could eat two more helpings.

My mother had plans for the rest of the afternoon, so she gathered her wraps and we left the house together.

We reached the middle of the block and were enveloped in the stinging acid aroma of vinegar from the pickle factory on the corner of Fillmore and Fulton streets. I had walked ahead. My mother stopped me and said, "Baby."

I walked back to her.

"Baby. I've been thinking and now I am sure. You are the greatest woman I've ever met."

My mother was five feet four inches to my six-foot frame.

I looked down at the pretty little woman, and her perfect makeup and diamond earrings, who owned a hotel and was admired by most people in San Francisco's black community.

She continued, "You are very kind and very intelligent and those elements are not always found together. Mrs. Eleanor Roosevelt, Dr. Mary McLeod Bethune, and my mother—yes, you belong in that category. Here, give me a kiss."

She kissed me on the lips and turned and jaywalked across the street to her beige and brown Pontiac. I pulled myself together and walked down to Fillmore Street. I crossed there and waited for the number 22 streetcar.

My policy of independence would not allow me to accept money or even a ride from my mother, but I welcomed her wisdom. Now I thought of her statement. I thought, Suppose she is right. She's very intelligent and she often said she didn't fear anyone enough to lie to him, so suppose she is right. Imagine, I really might be somebody. Imagine.

At that moment, when I could still taste the red rice, I decided the time had come when I should cut down on dangerous habits like smoking, drinking, and cursing.

Imagine, I might really become somebody.

Red Rice

SERVES 8

½ pound thick sliced bacon
1 cup chopped onions
½ cup chopped red bell peppers
2 cups canned tomatoes
One 6-ounce can tomato paste

Dash of freshly ground black pepper
½ teaspoon salt
4 cups cooked white rice
2 cups water

Fry bacon in a large skillet on medium heat until brown, stirring with fork. Add onions and peppers. Cover and cook for 2 to 3 minutes. Remove lid and add remaining ingredients; mix well. Bring to boil, about 3 minutes. Stir vigorously, cover again, and cook over very low heat for about 15 minutes until rice and liquid are totally mixed.

Roasted Capon

SERVES 4

One 2–3-pound capon
Juice of 1 lemon
1 cup water
4 tablespoons (½ stick) butter
Salt and freshly ground black
    pepper, to taste

1 unpeeled Granny Smith apple,
    cored and cut into pieces
1 stalk celery, cut into pieces

Preheat oven to 350°F.

Wash capon in lemon juice mixed with water. Pat dry, and rub butter over capon. Liberally salt and pepper capon outside and inside. Place apple and celery in capon cavity.

Make aluminum foil tent, and place over capon. Bake for 1 hour, periodically basting with juices in pan. Remove foil. Reduce oven to 325°F, and bake for 30 more minutes.

Good Banana, Bad Timing

T R. MANSFIELD WAS SHORT and mean and lean. He was mostly bones, with no spare meat anywhere on his body. His lemon-colored skin was pockmarked as a result of childhood chicken pox. He was literate, but just barely.

I was nineteen years old and crazy for him. When I was not occupied fulfilling my duties as a short-order cook or selling jazz music in a record store, I thought of nothing but T.R. Maybe it was his way of walking that captured and held me. He moved as if his chest and upper torso had no connection with the rest of his body and was pleased at the arrangement. Which meant that his hips swung with a giant promise of better things to come.

Or maybe it was his silence that intrigued me.

I had lived with or around my mother and brother who talked all the time. They could, at no notice at all, hold conversations on the Soviet Union, the Supreme Court, race relations, or whether salmon croquettes could adequately compete with fried pork chops.

I cannot remember T.R. ever initiating a discussion, and his rejoinders to my attempts to start a conversation were generally met with a throat clearing:

"Ah-hum. Great."

Or:

"Ah-hum-rum. Yeah."

Or:

"Ah-hum-rum. No."

I visited him in his rented room twice a week and always left happier and more at peace than when I arrived. I thought he was equally pleased. Of course with his inveterate silence, I could not be expected to know otherwise.

One evening, however, when I knocked at his door, a woman answered. I stood in amazement as the door opened and a short, very plain, light-skinned, plump woman twenty years my senior said, "Come in. You must be Maya."

I walked into the room and remained silent. The woman continued. "We must have gotten our days mixed up. You usually come on Tuesdays and Fridays. I come on Mondays, Wednesdays, and Saturdays. What's today?" She looked at her watch, "Ooo, I'm running late. T.R. is in the bathroom. Well, we probably won't see each other again. Bye-bye."

My brain was in shock; there was a straitjacket around my body. I didn't think. I couldn't move.

T.R. came out of the bathroom, surprised to see me. He grumbled low, "What are you doing here?"

I could comprehend, but I still couldn't speak.

"You not due today. Today is for Daphne. She let you in?"

He had never said that much to me in our nine-month relationship.

"Come on in the kitchen." I followed him down the hall. He took a dessert from the refrigerator and placed large spoonfuls on two plates.

"Get a fork." He nodded toward a drawer and began to eat with the serving spoon. He was hard to understand at best, and now with his mouth full of bananas and custard and vanilla wafers I should not have understood a word. But I will never forget what he said or its impact on me.

"Daphne. Ever hear of a Negro woman named Daphne? She makes this for me once a month. Her grandmother was a white woman."

Everybody I knew had at least one white grandparent or great grandparent. No one thought it was something to brag about.

"I've been loving her a long time. She's too good for me and she's married, but she comes anyway. You look all stove up like you're mad. Wait now, I never promised you anything and I'm going to be with Daphne as long as she'll have me. So just wipe that stupid look off your face."

He had finished his pudding and was digging for more. I looked at the sweet. The custard was poorly made and was already weeping pure water, the bananas were brown from exposure, and the vanilla wafers were soggy. Then I looked at T.R. He was a slothful, ignorant, and arrogant fool.

I stood up and pushed my plate to him and walked out.

On the street, I realized I had not said one word from the moment I entered that house until I left.

I stopped at the supermarket on the way home. In my kitchen I began to make my own banana pudding. When it was finished and properly chilled, my son and I sat down and ate it.

Poor T.R., he never had—and now never would have—a chance to taste a truly great banana pudding. I ate his portion that night and with each morsel I knew I would never see him again.

Banana Pudding

SERVES 8

3/4 cup plus 1 tablespoon sugar
1/3 cup cornstarch
Pinch of salt
3 cups milk
8 eggs, separated

3 tablespoons butter
1 tablespoon vanilla extract
3 cups vanilla wafer cookies
4 ripe bananas, thinly sliced
1/2 teaspoon cream of tartar

Preheat oven to 350°F.

Combine 1/3 cup sugar, cornstarch, and salt in a large saucepan; stir until blended. Stir in milk. Cook over medium heat, stirring constantly until thickened and boiling; boil 1 minute, then remove from heat.

In small bowl whisk egg yolks, then whisk in about 1/2 cup of the hot custard until blended. Pour yolk mixture back into custard in saucepan; cook over medium heat, stirring, for 2 minutes. Stir in butter and vanilla until blended.

Place half the vanilla wafers on bottom of shallow 2-quart casserole. Top with layers of banana slices and custard. Repeat layering, ending with pudding.

Beat egg whites and 1/4 cup sugar in large mixing bowl at low speed until frothy. Add cream of tartar; increase speed to medium and gradually beat in remaining sugar. Beat until whites just hold stiff peaks.

Immediately spoon meringue over hot custard, being sure that meringue touches baking dish on all sides (this helps prevent it from shrinking). Transfer to oven and bake until golden, 20 minutes. Remove from oven and cool 1 hour. Refrigerate at least 4 hours before serving.

Ready-to-Wear Tripe

MY FRIEND SAM FLOYD was the most dapper, eloquently dressing man I ever knew. Had he lived during the flapper days, he would have been one of the first to wear spats. In another age, he would have sported a foulard or a four-in-hand. He certainly would have owned a derby and a fedora. In fact, somewhere in his crowded closet in his crowded apartment in New York's Greenwich Village, he did have a beret from Paris and a top hat for formal evenings out on the New York town.

In the 1960s, he wore Brooks Brothers suits, Van Huesen shirts, and Sulka silk ties. His shoes were custom-made.

In 1969, Sam and I flew out to California to visit my mother, who was the most elegant-dressing woman I ever knew. She wore Daché hats and Lilli Ann suits, Lillie Rubin dresses, and Daniel Green slippers. They admired and even liked each other. They were a match.

Sam and I were invited to dinner by a friend of my mother's, who declined to go. The date started to go bad from the first minute. Our host opened the door and invited us directly to the bar in his den. He told Sam that he shouldn't have dressed up. He added, "There's no one in my house you have to impress."

I knew he was being friendly. Sam was offended. Sam wouldn't have thought that what he was wearing was dress-up. He said, "I didn't really have to try to achieve this just to come to your house."

I knew Sam was just being Sam, but now the host was offended. Just as he was preparing his rejoinder, I stepped in.

"May we order drinks? I've got dust in my throat." That was the height of the evening.

In a half hour, the host had stopped speaking to Sam who retaliated by trying to drink the bar dry. Sam ordinarily drank one or two whiskeys before dinner and some wine with the meal. On that particular night, Sam had whiskey after whiskey, and when dinner was served he refused the wine, saying he would go out with whom he came in. He ordered another scotch.

I don't think he tasted the food, and as quickly as I could, still being courteous, I said our thanks and good-byes.

Just before he passed out in my car, Sam said, "I drank because that jerk bored me."

He lurched into my mother's house and straight into the guest room. In the morning I was having coffee when he came into the kitchen holding his head.

"I drank everything I could to get back at our host."

I said, "And he's feeling it this morning, poor thing."

Sam said, "Don't add insult to injury."

Mother entered, saying, "Only if it is deserved."

I looked at both people whom I loved and thought how much alike they were. They were separated by a generation and by gender, but at 9:00 A.M. both had showered and chosen expensive dressing gowns just to come to the kitchen.

I asked Sam to recount for my mother what he could remember of the night before. I headed back to my room. When I returned, my mother was laughing heartily.

"What you need is a cold beer now, and as soon as I can make it, some tripe. Some good red-hot tripe and white rice! Or I can make the Mexican *menudo*."

Sam said, "I only know how to cook tripe à la mode de Caen." He pronounced the dish with a French accent.

My mother asked, "What?"

He started to tell her.

She said, "Wait, let me change. I'll be right back, and I'll cook my kind of tripe and you can tell me your recipe."

She went back to her room. Sam took his beer and disappeared, and I returned to my room.

I smelled onions frying and I followed the aroma to the kitchen. My mother, dressed in white, was stirring onions in a skillet.

Within minutes Sam entered, also in white. They looked at each other and laughed.

Sam said, "The beer saved my life. I'll have another."

Mother said, "Why don't you make us a few dry martinis? We'll eat soon."

I asked, "You cooked tripe that fast?"

"I used my pressure cooker, but it doesn't take as long as it used to now that they process tripe. They clean it and then precook it."

We sat at the table suffused in delicious aroma. Suddenly Sam's sleeve was caught on the martini glass and it tipped into his plate of tripe; then his plate slipped over onto my mother's lap. We all jumped. Sam apologized. Mother went to the sink.

I said, "Let's go to your bathroom and get some water on it immediately." We rushed to her room. When she had immersed her slacks and shirt in the basin she chose another white set and we walked back into the kitchen.

Sam Floyd had cleaned the table and put on a fresh tablecloth. We all had new plates.

Sam said, "I'm rarely clumsy enough to ruin someone else's clothes. And on only one other occasion have I spilled tomato sauce on my own self."

We sat down and enjoyed the food. Mother said, "This is good hangover food. Never fails."

Just as we finished eating, Sam tipped his plate. Red sauce spilled onto his summer white outfit.

My mother said, "You clever thing, you did that on purpose."

Sam swore he didn't plan to pour tripe on his clothes and maybe he didn't, but I know with that accident he made my mother his friend for life.

Tripe à la Mode de Caen

SERVES 4 TO 6

2 pounds fresh tripe
Bouquet Garni (p. 8)
3 carrots, peeled and diced
3 Spanish onions, diced
2 stalks celery, diced
3 cloves garlic, diced
¼-pound diced salt pork, cut into large pieces
4 bay leaves

10 black peppercorns
1 pig's foot
1 soup bone, pork, cracked
1 teaspoon salt
1 cup water
2 cups dry white wine
2 jiggers gin

Preheat oven to 350°F.

Wash tripe, and cut into bite-size cubes. Put all dry ingredients into large earthenware pot. Pour in water, wine, and gin. Cover tightly and bake for 5 hours. Remove from oven, and discard pig's foot, soup bone, and Bouquet Garni. Serve with crusty French bread.

Red Tripe with White Rice

SERVES 4 TO 6

2 pounds fresh tripe

2 tablespoons vegetable oil

1 small onion, sliced

Two 28-ounce cans tomatoes

One 6-ounce can tomato paste

2 cloves garlic, minced

Salt and freshly ground black
pepper, to taste

Red pepper flakes, to taste

4 to 6 cups hot cooked white rice

Wash tripe and cut into 1-inch pieces. Put in pot with water to cover, and simmer for 1½ hours. Drain, and pat dry.

In large skillet, sauté oil, onion, tomatoes, tomato paste, and garlic. Add tripe. Simmer 1 hour, or until tender. Season with salt, pepper, and red pepper flakes. Serve with rice.

Menudos
(tripe stew)

SERVES 8

5 pounds tripe
1 large beef soup bone
4 cloves garlic, chopped
3 teaspoons salt
2 cups chopped onions
1 teaspoon ground coriander
2 tablespoons chili powder (or more,
   to taste) or one 4-ounce can
   chopped green chilies

1½ quarts water
One 29-ounce can whole hominy
Juice of 1 lemon
1 tablespoon chopped fresh cilantro

Wash tripe, and cut into ½-inch-wide strips.

Place tripe, soup bone, garlic, salt, onions, coriander, chili powder, and water in a large pot. Simmer for 6 hours, or until tripe is tender, adding more water if necessary. Add hominy, lemon juice, and cilantro, and cook over medium to high heat for 30 minutes. Remove soup bone, and serve immediately.

M.J. and the Doctor and Mexican Food

.

THE HANDSOME DOCTOR CARED inordinately for tamales, and my friend-sister, the beautiful Mary Jane, called M.J., cared for the doctor. He had been the senior surgeon when Mary Jane was taken into a hospital with a life-threatening emergency. In hours, following the diligent application of his medical know-how, her life was saved and her principal savior was a handsome, young, dashing, unmarried doctor.

She returned home and used gargantuan control to keep herself from calling the doctor. Much to her delight, after a week he telephoned her and telephoned her and telephoned her until she agreed to go out with him. The courtship started slow and remained slow. The doctor was steady, but his ardor never heated up to the degree that M.J. wanted so that she could know the level of his commitment.

One day she invited me to visit. She lived in Santa Monica on the ground floor in a generous apartment of a building she owned. Her living room was rich with antique furniture, and the paintings of John Biggers, Elizabeth Catlett, and Samella Lewis hung on her walls.

M.J. was a rich-cream-colored woman with green-gray eyes and an electric personality. She told me that the doctor was coming for dinner and that she had an incredible recipe for tamales. Her smile of satisfaction was just comfortably one grin away from a smirk.

When I probed, she said her suitor loved Mexican food and he thought only some California Mexicans and a few Texas Mexicans could prepare tamales properly. She said whenever he was near a Mexican restaurant that served tamales, he was like a runaway horse. She had seen him pull up and halt and all but paw the ground at its door.

M.J. had bought all the ingredients to make dozens of her beloved's delight. She knew I cooked Mexican food often and she wanted me to see that everything went off well. I sat on a kitchen stool as she made arroz con pollo, refried beans, guacamole, salsa, carne Colorado, and, finally, the vaunted tamales. Her entire house was filled with the culinary perfumes of Guadalajara and Oaxaca and Jalisco.

The doctor entered the living room, but when we were introduced he could hardly concentrate enough to complete the simplest social pleasantries of "How are you?" and "Well, and you?"

I watched as his nostrils twitched from side to side, trying to ascertain if the aromas he thought he encountered were really there. He asked M.J. if she had sent out for Mexican food. She told him she had cooked the dinner. He asked what was on the menu. She answered, "Guacamole, chips, salsa, arroz con pollo," and so forth. She listed all the dishes except the much-adored tamales.

With each mention of food his smile widened and his body seemed to wave. He said, "If you had told me, I could have picked up some tamales. I was near the café."

She said, "Maybe we'll make do tonight. Maya is eating with us. Will you make drinks?"

The doctor surprised me. He was familiar enough with M.J.'s house to know where the liquor was kept and where to find highball glasses. She had not told me everything.

M.J. had set the table with colorful linens and Mexican plates. When she served the beans and rice, the carne Colorado, and the chicken and rice, the doctor spoke from the depth of a deep enchantment. "You made this? You yourself?"

As she headed toward the kitchen, she motioned me to sit down. I did so.

"Who would have thought that a smart and pretty woman like you could cook like this? This table looks like the real thing. If you had told me, I could have picked up some tamales."

She walked in carrying a plate filled with the doctor's dream comestibles. When he saw the platter he lost all sense of propriety. He plucked a tamale and put it on his plate. When he unwrapped the hot savory from the cornhusks, his face was a study in hope and apprehension. The long cornmeal tamale lay on his plate, and he waited a few seconds just in case it wasn't as good as he wished. Then he lifted his fork and cut a bite and put it in his mouth.

As the flavored cornmeal and the seasoned meat filling melted, he began to smile. Then the smile widened and he started to laugh. He made no eye contact, so he wasn't sharing the laughter. He was just enjoying himself with himself. When he finished the tamale, he looked at M.J. Looked at her as if he had never really seen her. Looked at her and realized that this woman who pleased him in many other ways could also cook tamales to make his heart stand still.

I was not at all surprised when M.J. told me that later that night he said he wanted to talk about a longtime commitment.

Tamales de Maíz con Pollo
(green cornhusk tamales with chicken filling)

MAKES 1 DOZEN TAMALES

2 whole chicken breasts
2 tablespoons vegetable oil
½ cup minced onions
2 cloves garlic, minced
¼ cup fresh parsley
½ cup fresh cilantro
¼ teaspoon cayenne pepper

1 teaspoon salt
Freshly ground black pepper, to
   taste
1¾ cups masa
1 cup warm water
¼ cup lard
24 fresh cornhusks

Wash chicken breasts, and cut from bone. Slice chicken into pencil-thin strips.

In large sauté pan, sauté chicken in oil for 15 minutes, or until done, and then remove from oil.

Sauté onions and garlic in oil until translucent. Return chicken to sauté pan, and add parsley, cilantro, cayenne pepper, and ½ teaspoon salt, and season with black pepper. Set aside to cool.

In heavy pot, mix together masa, water, remaining salt, and lard, and stir and cook over medium heat until very creamy and smooth, about 20 to 25 minutes. Cool to room temperature.

Trim the thick bottom part from cornhusks and wash well, removing any silk. For each tamale, take 2 cornhusks, pointed part at top, and paste together at one side with some of the masa mixture. This makes the husk wider. Now spread 1 tablespoon of the masa mixture on the inside about 1 inch from the bottom and extending about 2 inches up the husk. Top with 2 teaspoons of the filling. Fold husk around filling, paste with a little more masa, and then fold bottom toward top, making envelopes. Tie together with kitchen twine.

Stand up in a steamer, and steam for 1 hour. Tamales may be frozen and reheated over steam.

❦

Saving Face
and Smoking
in Italy

❧ ✦ ❧

THE ROCKEFELLER FOUNDATION's Study and Conference Center was a large mansion snuggled into the hills above Bellagio, Italy. Fifteen artists at a time from around the world were invited to the enclave. Selected artists with companions had to make their way to Milan airport, and then magically they were swept up by tender arms and placed in a lap of luxury that few popular movie stars or rich corporate chiefs even dreamed existed. A chauffeured car picked up the invitees and drove them carefully fifty miles north to Bellagio. There they were deposited at the Center, which stood atop a high hill. Its buildings were low-slung and meandered over carefully tended acres only a few miles from the Swiss border. Within those elegant walls, forty-eight employees cared for thirty guests and the retreat center's director and wife. Each artist had a commodious suite.

Once ensconced in this graciousness, the artists were informed of the regimen. Breakfast was ordered nightly and served each morning by footmen. Lunch was served informally at midday. Artists could sit at will in a casual dining room and choose food from an elaborate buffet. The time could have been passed off as an ordinary lunch save that each table sported a handwritten menu of foods offered and the company was served at the buffet table by the uniformed head waiter and the tailored butler.

The artists were addressed as *dottore*, which meant that their scholarship was respected. They were told that dinner was formal, and that was an understatement. Dinner was an event of meticulous structure. Guests were expected to dress each night and were directed where to sit by a placement, which lay on a hall table at the door of the drawing room. There must have been an exemplary social statistician in the Center's employ because in the four weeks when I was a resident, no one ever sat twice between the same two people.

Jessica Mitford and I were invited and found ourselves to be the only female artists. We had brought along our husbands, Robert Treuhaft and Paul du Feu, but the staff, so unused to female scholars, could not bring themselves to address us as they addressed the thirteen male scholars. So they called us *signora* and our husbands *dottore*.

One evening during a lull in the ten or twelve conversations plying the table, the director reminded the guests that Thanksgiving was approaching. He then asked if anyone had a good recipe for roast turkey and corn bread dressing. I waited, but no one moved. I said, "I do. I have a recipe." I spoke it before I thought.

Everyone beamed at me except my husband, Jessica, and Robert. In a second, their faces told me I had done the wrong thing. Company never volunteers, never offers. Nonetheless, the director said the butler would come to my suite mid-morning to collect the recipe.

I broke my writing schedule to recall and write the recipe. I handed the missive to the butler. Within minutes he returned and said the chef wanted to see the *dottore* who had sent him the recipe. I followed him down a flight of dark stairs and, without a hint of change to come, stepped suddenly into a vast noisy, hot, brightly lit kitchen, where a fleet of white uniformed cooks were stirring steaming pots and sizzling pans. The butler guided me over to meet the head chef, who wore a starched white toque. His surprise at seeing me let me know that he had expected Dottore Angelou to be a white male, and, instead, a six-foot-tall daughter of Africa stood before him ready to answer his questions. He did shake my hand, but he then turned his back rather rudely and shouted to another cook, "Come and talk to this woman. I don't have the time."

The second cook tried his English, but I told him we could speak Italian. He said, "Signora, we want to follow your recipe, but we have never made corn bread or corn bread dressing. We need your help."

I asked for cornmeal, only to be offered polenta. I asked for baking powder and was told they didn't even know what that was. When I described the work of baking powder, I was shown a large slab of moist yeast. The polenta was an orange powdery meal many times brighter than American yellow cornmeal.

During the Easter seasons, my mother always used yeast to make hot cross buns. I figured I could use it as the riser for my corn bread.

I gave my jacket to the butler and listed the other ingredients I needed. He put men to work, and in seconds I was able to put a pan of polenta corn bread into a hot oven and the turkey's neck, gizzard, liver, and wingtips to boil. I added celery, onions, a stick of cinnamon, and garlic to the pot.

When the bread came from the oven, hot and smoking, the head chef was standing near me. We both looked at the orange brown crust. His eyes widened. He said, "*Bella.*"

I said, "This is the bread my people eat."

The chef asked, "Who are your people?"

I answered, "African Americans. My ancestors came from Africa to America."

The chef said, "Every person in America except the Indians had ancestors who came from some other place."

I couldn't argue that.

He asked, "What makes you different from other Americans?"

I said, "My skin is black. That tells me and everyone who sees me who I am."

He raised his voice. "Roberto, Roberto, come."

A small dark-skinned cook came from the rear of the kitchen.

The chef said, "Here is Roberto. He is from Sicily, but because of his color should I call him an Afro-Italian?"

There was a burst of loud laughter. We had been speaking in Italian and everyone had heard our conversation and enjoyed the fact that the chef was putting me on.

I decided to stop the razzing and get on with the cooking. I quickly diced an onion and sautéed it in a large pan. I drained the stock and mixed some with the onion and crumbled corn bread in a large bowl. No one offered to help me, so I took the raw turkey and stuffed it with dressing. I laced the turkey's cavity and placed it into a roasting pan. I cut the oven down and set the turkey to roast.

I finely diced another onion and sautéed it and made gravy using the cut-up meat and the rest of the stock. I put a drop of the gravy on my thumb and tasted it for seasoning.

When I looked up, I realized the chef had been watching me for the past twenty minutes. His face told me he had been watching with approval.

He asked, "Would you like a smoke?"

I said, "Yes."

His nod told me to follow him. He shouted to the cooking staff, "Watch her sauce, and keep an eye on the turkey in the oven."

We walked out into an alley. He gave me a strong French cigarette and lighted his own and mine. He breathed in deeply and exhaled loudly, and although he never said a mumbling word I knew his invitation to me to join him in a smoke was his way to show his approval.

That night when the exclusive intellectual assemblage had gathered around the dining table, the chef entered followed by his sous-chef, who carried a fine brown turkey.

The sous-chef lifted the platter and bowed to the chef, who gave a small bow, then reached out his right hand to me and asked me to stand. All the scholars and their mates and the director applauded the turkey, the chef, and me.

I learned that day that a respect for food and its preparation could obliterate distances between sexes, languages, oceans, and continents.

Roasted Turkey

One 15–17-pound turkey	Corn Bread Stuffing (p. 118)
1 tablespoon salt	½ cup melted butter

Preheat oven to 325°F. Wash turkey thoroughly, and pat dry.

Rub turkey's neck and body cavities with salt. Lightly fill body cavity with Corn Bread Stuffing. Tie legs together with string. Stuff neck cavity lightly with stuffing. Draw neck skin over cavity to the back, and fasten with a skewer. Fasten wings behind back by bending tip ends under.

The turkey can be roasted in open pan or closed roaster, or wrapped in foil. Open-pan method is preferable and is described here.

Place turkey, breast side up, on wire rack in shallow pan. Insert roasting thermometer between thigh and body, avoiding bone.

Cover bird with cheesecloth dipped in melted butter. If cheesecloth dries during cooking time, spoon some of the drippings in pan over it.

Roast until thermometer registers 190°F, or until drumsticks can be moved up and down easily. When bird is done, remove cloth. Place turkey on a large hot platter. Let stand for about 20 minutes before carving, so the meat will absorb its own juices.

Corn Bread Stuffing

SERVES 8 TO 10

Turkey neck
Turkey wingtip
Turkey gizzard
Turkey liver
1 teaspoon salt
3 tablespoons vegetable oil
2 stalks celery, diced

1 small onion, diced
1 pan cooked corn bread, cooled (use
    Crackling Corn Bread recipe on
    p. 27, but omit cracklings)
4 tablespoons dried sage
1 tablespoon dried oregano
3 large eggs

Preheat oven to 350°F. Grease 9 × 9-inch baking pan.

Place washed turkey parts in 4-quart pot. Add enough water to cover. Add salt, boil, and then let cool.

Into a large sauté pan, put oil, celery, and onion, and sauté until tender. Let cool.

Crumble corn bread, and add sage, oregano, and sautéed onion-and-celery mixture.

Strain turkey parts, reserving broth. Chop neck, gizzard, and liver meats. Pour broth and chopped meats into corn bread mixture. Add eggs, and mix well.

Add some stuffing to turkey cavity and some to neck cavity (see p. 117). Spoon rest of stuffing into greased baking pan, and cook for 30 minutes.

Haute Cuisine
à la
Tabasco

MISS ANNABELLE ROSS WAS A SWEETLY sympathetic figure. In her sixties she was prematurely old and had the manner of what southerners call a settled lady. Yet she was a coloratura soprano with *Porgy and Bess*, which meant that she was a member of a highly trained, largely young cast of opera singers who could, and did, belt out the blues just as easily as they sang bel canto Respighi, Verdi, and the art songs of Purcell.

She was not the only older singer in the group, but the others over age fifty entertained themselves by playing stud poker, keno, and cut-throat pinochle, which they called pig knuckles. They also drank their portion of gin martinis, Black & White scotch, and Jack Daniel's whiskey.

Miss Ross played no games, nor did she drink or smoke. Until she was called on stage she sat closed inside her wall of niceness looking lost and very sad. I was twenty-six years old, and because I doted on my grandmother who doted on me I had a tender feeling for older women, the grandmotherly type.

Porgy and Bess was appearing at the Teatre Wagram in Paris, and I was the principal dancer and sang the role of Ruby. I doubled singing blues and calypso in nightclubs after the curtain fell at the opera.

I watched Miss Ross and wondered how I could raise her spirits. One early evening I went to Fouquets Restaurant on the Champs Elysées. I asked to speak to the maître d'hôtel. My presence shocked him. He had not been summoned by many six-foot-tall African American girls.

He asked me in French if I had ever visited a first-class restaurant. I replied, "No, but I am young and certainly I will do so in my life."

He nodded. I told him about Miss Ross. I described her age and her loneliness. I said I didn't have much money but that I'd like to bring her to his restaurant for one great dinner. It might be her first and last time to have a superb French meal. His countenance softened and he called two waiters and repeated my story. I was invited inside to a table where the four of us sat down and pored over the menu.

The experts chose a pâté to start, then molded eggs polignac for our second course. We would be served veal medallions for our entrée. A waiter showed me my bill. I was amazed at how little I was charged. Then I realized the maître d' had reduced the price because of my story.

On the designated night, Miss Ross and I got out of a taxi. We had dressed in our best and made ourselves up to go out for a fancy Parisian evening.

We were greeted at the door as if we were royalty. Every waiter made his way by to say hello. Obviously our tale had been told to the entire staff. The maître d' seated us and within seconds there was a crowd of waiters around the table bringing still and carbonated water, serving bread and butter, and placing salt and pepper and mustard.

To my surprise, Miss Ross was a refreshing dinner guest. She told charming stories and had a ready repartee. When the meal was served, I sat at attention to observe how she would enjoy her two-star dinner.

She tasted the pâté. She said she really liked that. She had long been partial to liverwurst but preferred it on white bread with a thick slab of raw onions and lots of mayonnaise. The molded eggs polignac also delighted Miss Ross. The staff sent approving nods around the room as the veal was served because Miss Ross made a slight smacking sound and rubbed her hands together.

She tasted the meat. "Now this is good." She took another bite of the medallions. The nearest waiter recorded her approval and sent her reaction to his colleagues.

Miss Ross said, "This is close to perfect. These people can truly cook."

I was reminded of my mother's actions in restaurants. When she was particularly pleased with a dinner, she would send a glass of wine to the chef. I didn't think I had enough money for that gesture, but I was floating in self-admiration until I heard Miss Ross say, "All this needs is a little Tabasco."

I looked at her, knowing that I had to dissuade her from asking the waiter to bring her the spicy sauce. But as I turned, Miss Ross was extricating a slim bottle of Tabasco from her purse.

"This is going to make this meat right perfect. I mean perfect."

She shook the bottle over the medallions, then she closed the bottle and placed it back in her purse.

The waiters were horrified. Although stricken, at least they were able to move around the restaurant. The maître d'hôtel was so shocked, however, that he disappeared from the floor, and I confess I wanted to join him.

I have grown a little since that incident. I've come to believe that each diner should be free to flavor her dish as she wants it. For no matter how wonderfully trained the chef, no matter how delicate his or her sensitivity, taste buds are as individual as fingerprints. Mine are mine and yours are yours and *vive la différence.*

I offer you here my veal medallions recipe. BYOT (bring your own Tabasco). It's optional.

Veal Medallions

SERVES 6

1½ pounds thin veal escallops
All-purpose flour
3 tablespoons butter
1 tablespoon olive oil
Salt and freshly ground black
    pepper, to taste

2 cups mushroom buttons
1 cup fruity white wine
¼ cup chopped fresh parsley

Dust veal with flour, and in large sauté pan brown quickly on both sides in 1½ tablespoons butter mixed with oil. Remove veal, and season with salt and pepper. Keep warm.

Sauté mushrooms until soft. Cover with ¾ cup wine, and continue cooking until the wine is reduced to half.

Add veal to mushrooms on medium heat. After 5 minutes remove veal to a hot platter.

Add the remaining wine to the pan. Add remaining butter. Bring to a boil, and then simmer for 4 minutes. Add parsley, and pour over the meat. Serve with steamed white rice.

Pâté

2 pounds goose or duck or chicken livers

1 teaspoon salt

½ teaspoon freshly ground black pepper

All-purpose flour

12 tablespoons (1½ sticks) soft butter

½ pound ground veal

1 cup diced onions

¼ teaspoon ground cinnamon

¼ teaspoon ground nutmeg

½ cup Rémy Martin cognac

1 cup chicken stock

Preheat oven to 350°F. Liberally butter 9 × 3-inch loaf pan.

Clean livers of all veins, gristle, and fat. Season with salt and pepper, and dust with flour.

In large sauté pan, melt 4 tablespoons (½ stick) butter, and place veal and livers in pan. Sauté on medium heat until done. (When no blood comes from the veal and livers, they are done.) Cool, and remove from pan to warm plate.

Put remaining butter into pan. Melt, and add onions. Sauté on medium heat until translucent. Let cool.

Purée livers, veal, and onions. Mix in cinnamon, nutmeg, and cognac, then chicken stock.

Pour mixture into loaf pan. Bake 30 minutes. Remove and cool. Place in refrigerator with another loaf pan holding two 15-ounce cans vegetables on top of pâté for 24 hours (to remove any air pockets in the baked mixture). Slice and serve cold.

Molded Eggs Polignac

SERVES 6

9 teaspoons butter, plus more for
 toast and garnish
6 truffle slices
6 large eggs

6 buttered toast rounds
2 teaspoons finely chopped fresh
 parsley

Preheat oven to 350°F.

Melt 1¹/₂ teaspoons butter in each of six small molds or ramekins. Lay a slice of truffle in the bottom of each mold. Break an egg into each mold, and set the molds in a pan of hot water. Bake for 8 to 10 minutes, or until the whites are set and the yolks a little soft.

Remove the molds from the hot water and let the eggs and truffles cool for a few minutes. Unmold each egg and truffle onto a small round of buttered toast, and garnish with melted butter and parsley.

English,
Please

THE LONDON DRAWING ROOM glowed beneath subdued lighting. Antique furniture showed its age gracefully, and our hostess, Sonia Orwell, was what she wanted to be: a picture of an upper-class hoyden.

I was introduced to the guests and told that they were great artists. One painter was the grandson of a famous psychiatrist, another painter had the same name as a renowned eighteenth-century English writer, and yet another was a trendy painter-photographer. Sonia shook her mane of blond hair and told them that I was writing a book.

The men gathered around me and asked pointed questions that seemed at odds in such amiable quarters.

"What on earth do you find in London that you don't have in the States?"

"Why do you come to England to write?"

"You can't escape racism, you know. English say all wogs begin at Calley."

True, I didn't know from his accent that his Calley meant the French town Calais, nor at that time did I know that the word *wog* meant "nigger," but I knew they were being hostile to me, so I responded in kind.

"I wanted to be in familiar surroundings. And you've just shown me there are as many ignoramuses here as there are in the United States. I didn't come here looking for anything. I brought everything I need with me. I know it is more blessed to give than to receive, so I'm willing to donate some of my wit to those who need it so badly."

Sonia shook her hair and said, "You've found a match!" The men laughed at my retorts.

We had become fairly friendly by the time we were asked to come downstairs to dinner.

We sat at a beautiful table festooned with personal nosegays at each plate.

The first course was an onion tart. I had never tasted anything better. I chewed slowly, registering each flavor. The shortness of the crust backed up the sweetness of caramelized onions. Voices intruded into my reverie.

"Maya, yes, Maya, what do you think of contemporary composers?"

"Yes. Like John Cage?"

I said, "Well, for me the emperor has no clothes. I think he is an impostor."

Each artist, and even Sonia, began to shout at me. "You can't call John Cage an impostor."

I remembered fifteen years earlier being an impoverished dancer. I saved every penny of my money so that I could attend a John Cage concert. I sat happily in the cheapest seat waiting for the artist so many people held as one of the important figures of twentieth-century art.

John Cage and a stagehand appeared carrying a record player. They plugged it into a socket and left the stage.

As the audience waited, there was a click and after a few seconds there was another click. Then another click. And another click.

I looked at the program and it read something like "Traffic Light at the Corner of Sixty-fifth and Park Avenue."

I left the theater hurriedly, pushing myself past people who were rapt in ecstasy over the sound of a traffic light clicking.

On the street, I was spitting mad. I had given up too many slices of pizza and ice-cream cones and subway rides to be so insulted.

I repeated at Sonia's table, "Yes, I think he is a charlatan and a poseur."

The company looked at me with disgust.

"Obviously conversation with you will be impossible."

"Anyone ignorant enough to call Cage a poseur is too ignorant for social exchange."

"Where did you find her, Sonia?"

Sonia came out of the kitchen carrying a tray that held a beautiful roast pork and baked apples. I stood up.

"Thank you, Sonia. I realize I have to be in Bangkok in half an hour."

She followed me upstairs and to her front door.

"Maya, they really like you. They think of you as an equal or they wouldn't have talked that way."

"I will never be their equal and they will never be mine."

I walked down her front stairs and into the London night.

I could have kicked myself for having wasted an evening. Then I thought I didn't really waste the evening. I did meet up with a great onion tart, and I had had the time to linger over it. And (I hoped) I could solve its mystery.

Onion Tart

SERVES 6

4 cups thinly sliced onions
3 tablespoons butter or bacon fat
2 cups heavy cream
3 large eggs, slightly beaten
1½ teaspoons salt

¼ teaspoon paprika
¼ teaspoon pepper
⅛ teaspoon ground nutmeg
9-inch pie shell, baked

Preheat oven to 450°F for 10 minutes.

Sauté onions in butter or bacon fat slowly until soft and golden.

Cool to room temperature. Add cream, eggs, salt, paprika, pepper, and nutmeg to onions, mix well, and turn into pie shell.

Bake for 10 minutes. Then reduce heat to 350°F, and bake for 30 minutes longer, or until knife blade inserted in the tart comes out clean.

＊

Sweet
Southern
Memories

I N THE MID-1960S, Los Angeles was friendly but unfocused for me. Thanks to Frances Williams, whom I had known years earlier, I had a place to stay but no job, and my money was slipping away.

I had sounded like a dunce at the employment agency.

The young, serious social worker asked, "What was your last job?"

"I sang calypso and blues in a supper club."

She made notes and then asked, "Where was that?"

"In Oahu, Hawaii, Waikiki."

Her eyes opened. "Why did you stop?"

"I realized I don't sing very well."

She caught a breath. "Ahem, okay. What did you do before that?"

"I was an administrative assistant at a university."

"Oh." For a moment she found relief. "So, you can type?"

"No, but I can file."

The relief vanished. "At what university did you work?"

"At the University of Ghana in West Africa."

The interviewer let the pencil fall from her fingers. "I don't have anything for you. You may be unemployable."

As was to be expected, Frances Williams knew someone who could offer me a job. She asked if I could cook.

I said, "I cook very well."

She asked, "Southern?"

I said, "Of course, but I don't really want a job as a cook."

She said, "No, that's not the job I'm looking at for you. Let me tell you about

Phil, who handles random research systems for large companies like Kellogg's and General Foods and Ivory Soap."

She said Phil had a publicity agency and was a good ole white boy from the South. He was so homesick that he would break down and cry if you mentioned fried chicken.

She said she would invite him to her house, and if I made a southern brunch, she was pretty certain he would give me a job. She asked, "Are you sure you can cook? I can't help you because that would be lying and lying won't help anybody in the end, and I tell the truth. Tell a lie and you'll never be finished scheming." That was Frances Williams's motto.

She offered to buy the brunch ingredients and said she'd call Phil and a few other friends so he wouldn't feel set up.

I said, "But we are setting him up."

"Not at all," she said, "unless you want to think I'm setting you up. Here's how I see it. My friends and I are going to find out if you can really cook. If so, and you cook southern, Phil is going to think he's waking up in a dream and you'll get a job. Friends of mine who haven't seen me or each other in months will have a great time."

I made a list for her. She asked, "No grits? You'll have a southern breakfast without grits?"

I said, "They won't be missed."

On Sunday morning, I went early to Frances's kitchen, and when everyone arrived I was sitting calmly in the living room, which was alive with the aromas of sage and caramelized brown sugar.

Frances introduced me to Phil. "She's just come from Africa." His face was a mask of disinterest. "But she's from the South." A little interest awakened his features.

"From where?"

I said, "A little hamlet in Arkansas, twenty-five miles from Texarkana."

He gave me a smile grudgingly. "You miss it, don't you?"

Frances spoke before I had to lie. "She's out here looking for a job, and she's so sweet she came over here and made our brunch. The whole thing."

I had his full attention. "What did you cook?"

I said, "Sausage and eggs."

He asked in a little boy's voice, "And grits?"

I said, "No," and the smile slid down to the floor. I quickly added, "I made spoon bread."

"Spoon bread. You said spoon bread? I haven't had spoon bread since I left Birmingham."

Seeing him so pleased delighted me. I added, "I make my own sausage, and we'll also have fried apples and homemade biscuits." His smile was so winning I could have hugged him.

Brunch was offered buffet-style. After Phil served himself, he sat alone on a window seat. I watched as his eyes visited each item on his plate. Only after he assured himself that he had seen what he thought he had seen did he begin to eat. He would put a forkful of food in his mouth and then he would seem to disappear. He slowly chewed his way back to his Alabama childhood.

Later I saw Frances and him talking out on the patio. When they came in, he headed straight to me.

"You can start on Monday. It doesn't pay much, but it's easy work. Fran says you are a writer. I just want you to give me your recipe for spoon bread and for biscuits and for sausage. Oh yeah, and for fried apples, too. Well, if you can write half as good as you can cook, you are going to be famous."

Spoon Bread

SERVES 6 TO 8

2 cups white cornmeal

1 cup all-purpose flour

4 teaspoons baking powder

2 teaspoons salt

1½ cups cold water

1 cup boiling water

2 tablespoons (¼ stick) butter, melted

2 large eggs, beaten

1½ cups milk

Preheat oven to 375°F. Butter a 2-quart casserole dish.

Sift together cornmeal, flour, baking powder, and salt. Stir in cold water. Add boiling water, and stir vigorously. Add remaining ingredients, and mix well. Pour into casserole dish. Bake for 1 hour, or until firm and browned. Serve at once.

Fried Apples

SERVES 6

6 Granny Smith apples

2 McIntosh apples

4 tablespoons (½ stick) butter

2 tablespoons brown sugar

1 cup water

½ teaspoon ground cinnamon

¼ teaspoon ground nutmeg

Quarter and core apples, but do not peel. Melt butter in large frying pan, and place apples skin side down in pan. Sprinkle with brown sugar, and add water. Add cinnamon and nutmeg, cover, and cook very slowly over low heat until tender and candied. Eat hot.

Homemade Biscuits

MAKES 1 DOZEN BISCUITS

3 cups all-purpose flour
5 teaspoons baking powder
½ teaspoon salt

½ cup Crisco shortening
1 cup milk

Preheat oven to 350°F.

Sift flour, baking powder, and salt together. Cut in shortening until mixture resembles coarse cornmeal. Add milk, using more if needed, to make a soft dough.

Roll out dough on floured board to ¾-inch thickness. Cut into 2-inch rounds. (If biscuit cutter is not at hand, use water glass dipped in flour.) Bake on well-greased cookie sheet for 25 minutes (longer if you want them browner).

Sausage

SERVES 6

2 pounds raw pork
¼ pound pork fat
2 teaspoons salt
1 teaspoon sage

1 teaspoon red pepper flakes
1 teaspoon freshly ground
  black pepper

Grind pork with pork fat. Mix salt, sage, red pepper flakes, pepper, and ground meat. Using 2 heaping tablespoons of meat each, roll into balls, then flatten. Fry in medium-hot skillet until no blood is visible.

Fowl
Communication

J ESSICA MITFORD, WHO WAS CALLED DECCA, was a Briton transplanted among the hoi polloi in Oakland, California. To be more precise, Decca Mitford was an English aristocrat who once chose to become a card-carrying member of the Communist Party and live in a working-class town in northern California.

She and her lawyer husband, Robert Treuhaft, later left the party because they concluded that the organization was reneging on some of the high and lofty political and ethical ideals that had first appealed to them.

Bob and Decca lived in a commodious, rambling 1920s California bungalow, where they entertained celebrities and others, from the legendary blues singer Leadbelly to the odd felon on the run.

Bob was always the cook, specializing in the very best Boston baked beans, duck pâté, and butterflied roast leg of lamb. Decca mostly tidied up.

Decca and Bob's group was planning a large gala, and as preparatory chores were appointed most people thought Decca couldn't be much help in the kitchen, so she was asked to order the chickens, which more experienced members would then cook.

Decca telephoned the number she had been given for the chickens.

"I'd like to order fifty frying chickens to be delivered to a social hall on Wednesday at ten o'clock A.M."

"Do you want them dressed or undressed?"

She said, "Undressed of course."

Decca told me, "You must know that banqueting is also a part of the struggle."

She went to the meeting hall on Wednesday and was utterly shocked to see fifty chickens delivered with feathers, heads, necks, and feet attached.

She shouted at the deliverymen, "Why do they have all these things on them? I told you I wanted them undressed."

She was informed that in poultry parlance *undressed* meant with all the things on them and in them.

Decca called headquarters and told her story. She asked if there were any communists who knew how to dress a chicken.

Within an hour, chicken pluckers and cleaners were at the hall. They immediately began defeathering and disemboweling the chickens. When Decca saw the amount of work that was necessary, she was stricken with gratitude. No one had ever seen her so apologetic.

"Listen, I'm very sorry. And all of this brought about by my saying undressed rather than dressed."

One of the pluckers said, "You couldn't have known, Decca. You speak English. We speak American. We also speak poultry. What you do, you do so well. You deserve to take one of these chickens home fully dressed."

She accepted the chicken. She brought it home and opened a bottle of white wine, and quickly drank one half. Without benefit of recipe, she began to cook. She put the chicken into a casserole pot along with celery, onions, seasoning, and the rest of the wine.

She called her husband and told him what she had done, and she went to bed. When Bob came home, he removed the pot and opened it. The chicken was beautifully cooked.

From that time, I have cooked that dish following Decca's recipe and served it once a month, both to my delight and to the pleasure of my guests.

It is still called Decca's Chicken, Drunkard Style.

Decca's Chicken, Drunkard Style

SERVES 6

First, drink 1 glass of wine.

1 chicken (about 3 pounds), cut into pieces
1 stalk celery, chopped
1 medium onion, chopped
1 carrot, peeled and chopped
2 cloves garlic, minced

½ cup water
2 teaspoons salt
½ bottle Chardonnay
Freshly ground black pepper, to taste

Preheat oven to 375°F.

Wash chicken. Put all ingredients into a large, heavy pot, and place in oven. Bake for 2 hours. Serve hot.

If you want thick gravy, remove chicken and vegetables from pot. Add 3 tablespoons cornstarch and ¾ cup water to hot broth. Put back into oven until thickened to desired consistency.

Bob's Boston Baked Beans

SERVES 6

2 cups dried Great Northern beans
1/4 pound lean salt pork
1 medium onion, diced
1 teaspoon salt

1/2 cup light molasses
1/2 teaspoon dried mustard
1 tablespoon sugar

Pick over beans, discarding stones or debris. Rinse beans, then soak overnight in enough water to cover.

Next morning, drain beans. Fill large pot with water, and add beans, pork, onion, and salt. Boil covered until semitender, about 45 to 50 minutes. Watch carefully—water must be kept above beans in pot.

Preheat oven to 300°F.

Mix remaining ingredients with beans. Pour into a casserole dish. Bury pork in beans, leaving rind exposed. Cover. Bake for 4 hours.

M. F. K. Fisher
and a
White Bean
Feast

❧ ✦ ❧

Sonoma, california, was a working town. Some camera-wielding tourists did visit on weekends, lured by the romance of the ancient Spanish missions and proximity of the local vineyards, but the town was so busy serving itself there was no time for it to become quaint, precious, or twee.

Cattle ranchers, vineyard workers, farmers, and shop owners used the streets and the parks as if they were extensions of their own homes. Teachers, professors, members of the religious community, and artists held proprietary feelings about the town. Aging hippies mixed with young malcontents; singers from the local chorale walked shoulder to shoulder with the rich local barons. During the golden seventies we moved from Berkeley to Sonoma. My husband and I had come to know the area by visiting our friends David Bouverie and M. F. K. Fisher, who lived there.

The town liked itself so much that it gave itself a party once a year. The summer fête was called the Ox-Roast. During the roast weekend, locals would crowd the town square, bringing their own victuals. (I don't remember seeing anyone actually eating the ox that was cooked on a spit, which took ten strong men to turn.)

We moved to Sonoma during that annual celebration, and I phoned Mary Frances to learn if she planned to visit the public picnic. She told me she would not be coming that year.

Then I asked her to dinner in our new place. When I added that my husband would come and pick her up, she said she would be happy to come.

There was a chic cookery shop on the town square. The two men who owned the store, Gene and Dick, matched it perfectly.

They had an eastern vogue about them. They welcomed me warmly when I entered the shop. They'd heard that I was moving to Sonoma and they were happy to help me.

They supposed my pots and pans were still in boxes, and they had made a list of the best restaurants in town, which they were sure I would need. Most of my cookware was indeed still packed away, but I explained that I had invited someone for dinner that evening and that I would need to buy a few pots to use that night.

"You are cooking in pots you have not tried? Maybe your guests are not too keen on cuisine and they will never know."

I said, "My guest is very keen on cuisine. Her name is M. F. K. Fisher."

"You mean . . . you don't mean . . . Mary Frances Kennedy Fisher?"

I said, "Yes."

Dick looked at me as if I were Julia Child and had just flown in the door with saucepans for wings.

"You are going to cook for M. F. K. Fisher?"

I said, "She has to eat also."

"We've asked her to have dinner, but we've taken her to restaurants. We would never cook for her."

Gene asked, "What do you plan to cook?"

I said, "A cassoulet."

They both laughed out loud. I defended my choice. "I know that fall is a great season for cassoulet, but after all it is a peasant dish—so any season is great if you like beans and meat."

"Please let us know how Mary Frances enjoyed your dinner." They wore wry smiles as we said good-bye.

I began preparing the cassoulet, and my husband opened enough boxes for me to set a good table.

When he brought Mary Frances back, we had a trio of good stories, laughter, and good wine.

Mary Frances was easy with the chaos of my new house.

She said, "All new houses are the same. They search around a few months for their true personalities. This is an amiable space. I think you'll both be very happy here." We had an aperitif then went to the table.

I told her that the owners of the cookery shop were shocked that I would cook for her.

She reminded me of what had happened to her in Hollywood. She said that in the 1930s and 1940s she had written scripts in Hollywood but her prowess as a cook had preceded her. The glamorous stars had invited her to their Beverly Hills and Bel Air mansions for drinks and canapés, cocktails and hors d'oeuvres. She said she could smell dinner as it was being cooked, but hosts were so intimidated by her reputation that after drinks they would have their chauffeurs take her back to the hotel.

She said she would have given anything for a home-cooked hamburger or a decent omelet made in the kitchen of a friend.

I served the cassoulet with good Sonoma bread.

She spent a few quiet seconds savoring each flavor, but she was such an adept social guest that the conversation never lagged nor did the food get cold.

We took dessert, a simple flan, out by the swimming pool. She was the perfect guest. She left at the proper time, not too early, nor too late.

My husband took her home. When he returned, he said, "She really enjoyed the evening." I wasn't all that sure. I thought the beans had been a little mushy.

One week later I received a thank-you note with a few comments on the state of the world. After her signature, there was a P.S.:

"Dear Maya, thank you. That was the first honest cassoulet I have eaten in years."

Cassoulet

SERVES 8 TO 10

4 cups pea beans, washed and
 drained

2 quarts water

1 tablespoon salt

2 cloves garlic, mashed

2 carrots, peeled and quartered

2 medium onions, whole

Bouquet garni made of parsley,
 4 cloves, bay leaf, and thyme
 (see p. 8)

½ cup salt pork, diced

2 tablespoons duck or goose
 drippings or olive oil

1½ pounds lean boneless pork, cubed

1 pound boneless lamb, cubed

2 small Bermuda onions, chopped

1 cup chopped green onions (white
 and green parts)

1 cup thinly sliced celery

1 cup tomato sauce or juice

1 cup dry white wine

1 garlic sausage or Polish sausage,
 sliced into ¼-inch pieces

1 roasted duck or roasted goose,
 removed from bones and
 cut into bite-size pieces

1 roasted chicken, removed from
 bones and cut into bite-size
 pieces

Combine beans, water, and salt in large kettle. Let stand overnight, or boil for 2 minutes and let soak for 1 hour.

Add garlic, carrots, onions, bouquet garni, and salt pork, and bring to a boil. Simmer, covered, for 1 hour, skimming surface as needed.

Heat drippings in large skillet. Add pork and lamb, and brown on all sides over medium heat. Add to bean mixture.

In same skillet, sauté Bermuda onions, green onions, and celery until soft. Add tomato sauce and wine, and simmer for 5 minutes. Add to beans together with sausage. Simmer covered over low heat for 1 hour, or until beans and meats are tender. If necessary, add a little water to prevent scorching. Skim off excess fat. Discard bouquet garni.

Preheat oven to 350°F.

Transfer mixture to large casserole dish, and add pieces of duck and chicken. Bake covered for 30 minutes, stirring a couple times. Check occasionally for moisture; if necessary, add a little wine or water. Adjust seasoning. Serve hot.

From Pizza
to Claiborne
and Back

THE HOST SAID WE WERE EATING braised beef and potatoes. We knew she had an inordinate amount of false modesty and that in fact she had served us an exquisite *daube de boeuf* with potatoes Annette. Her dessert almost knocked us back from the dining table. Like fried ice cream, it was oxymoronic. She ended her splendid dinner by serving a cold lemon mousse with a baked meringue topping. We were floored.

We were an eclectic assemblage who had developed, without planning, a habit of cooking for each other once a month. At the end of each incredible meal (each host tried to outdo the last), the next cook would volunteer.

Everyone knew that I should be the next host, but I hesitated. How does one follow Auguste Escoffier or M. F. K. Fisher? I rolled my trepidation into a pill and swallowed it. "Come to me next month, I'll be ready."

My friends looked at me pityingly.

Once swallowed, the fear remained buried, and I tamped it further down with the knowledge that after all I was a good cook and I was in New York City where anything I thought I needed could be found. I toyed with duck galantine and sautéed veal with sherry and macadamia nuts. I considered a ten-boy lamb curry, placing ten relishes in my mind's eye: grated coconut, golden raisins, Major Grey's mango chutney, diced avocado, diced onion, tomatoes, fried onions, banana, cucumbers vinaigrette, and plain yogurt. Although no award of any kind was at stake, the competitive spirit among the circle of cooking friends was alive and kicking. I did not dare risk those dishes I'd thought of against the dinner we had just finished.

When the group came to my house, I fell back on my Arkansas upbringing. I gave them a black-eyed pea soup and southern fried chicken with homemade biscuits. For dessert I offered New Orleans pecan pie with a bourbon sauce. The food was a knockout, I had held on to my reputation as a peer among peers.

Bebe was a single parent who bragged in her heavy Uruguayan accent that she couldn't cook and wouldn't cook. She said she was raising her tall strapping teenage son, Bo, on dry cereal and milk in the morning, pizza and a salad for lunch, and the same thing for dinner. Her presence in our circle of writers who considered themselves to be gourmet cooks was inexplicable, but she did belong. She was a businesswoman and a writer who was very funny and interesting.

As we were having dessert, Bebe shocked us by saying, "Come to my apartment for dinner next month." We almost choked on our pecan pie.

"No, no. We know you don't know how to . . ."

"Really, I had planned to be in Bangkok that . . ."

"Oh, no, you shouldn't have to do this."

"Okay. We'll come and eat pizza and salad."

"I like a good pizza. A good pizza is a work of art . . ."

Bebe said, "No, we won't eat pizza. I will cook."

When the evening was over, everybody left laughing in their hands. Would we really be given take-out pizza for dinner and would she at least make the salad dressing at home?

Four weeks later, we met in the lobby of her building, still snickering.

"What do you think?"

"I brought my Tums."

"I brought Alka-Seltzer for everybody."

When we emerged from the elevator on her floor, the hall was redolent of mouthwatering aromas.

"At least somebody on her floor knows how to cook."

"Or maybe just someone in the building."

We laughed as Bebe opened the door, but our laughter ended when we entered her apartment. As we followed her to the living room, we knew that the aromas emanated from her kitchen. We were stunned. Her son, Bo, brought out a tray of drinks with a filled ice bucket, tongs, olives, and slices of lemon. We were invited to make our own drinks as Bebe disappeared into the kitchen. We could find nothing to say, so we offered blank faces to each other as we helped ourselves to libation. Bo emerged from the kitchen again, with a larger tray, which held oversized cups. He said "Gazpacho, please take one." The Spanish tomato soup was as cold as it should have been and rich with bite sizes of cucumber and finely chopped onion.

Many would-be cooks attempt to make gazpacho but conclude with horrific nonedible, nonpotable results. This one was as perfect a blend as any I had ever tasted. Bebe stayed in the kitchen as we chewed the crunchy vegetables and drank the beautifully flavored cold tomato soup.

Bo collected the empty cups and asked if we would sit to table. There were place cards. We knew Bebe hadn't been brought up in a barn, but nothing about her prepared us for this sophistication. After we were seated, she stepped into the dining room and announced, "Dinner is served." When she turned back into the kitchen, the smile on her face was sweet enough to rot teeth. She and Bo returned, placing on the table *petit pois* with pearl onions in a cream sauce, haricots verts in vinaigrette, and twice-baked potatoes and mushroom gravy. The pièce de résistance was a beef Wellington.

We stood and applauded and she joined in the admiring laughter. Each of us knew the complexity of building a beef Wellington. How the duxelles must be prepared while the loin is in the oven. How the loin must be cooling as the short pastry rests in the refrigerator. How the pâté must be at a spreadable consistency before the duxelles is patted in place. Bebe said she would love to tell us when we finished eating how a noncook had managed to bring off a four-star dinner.

We sat with small bowls of good commercial ice cream for dessert and she described her day. At 10 A.M., she telephoned *The New York Times* and asked to speak to food editor Craig Claiborne. She would not be pacified by his assistant. When Mr. Claiborne answered, Bebe accented her already heavy accent and, with her flair for dramatics, began to cry. "Mr. Claiborne, I am the wife of the Uruguay ambassador and I have invited eight couples of diplomats and two foreign vice presidents with their wives for dinner. This morning"—here a loud outburst of sobs—"my cook and his staff walked out in a huff. Oh my, Mr. Claiborne, I fear an international incident. I had the cook send out the menu, and I cannot possibly deliver." According to Bebe, Craig Claiborne asked what the menu was.

She replied, "Gazpacho, beef Wellington, *petit pois*, twice-baked potatoes, and haricots verts."

She told him she had all the ingredients and a grown daughter who could help her. He assured her that he would keep the telephone open all day and would walk her through each dish. All she had to do was follow his instructions to the letter.

According to her, he did keep the telephone open, and from the success of the dinner, she certainly followed his instructions.

As we left her apartment, she said, "I did this to prove to you unbearable egotists that cooking is no big thing. After we eat up all the leftovers, Bo and I will be back to pizza and salad. I'm not a cook and look what I was able to do."

I think Bebe is a great cook. No one knew it then.

I believe one can be born a great cook, achieve the status of a great cook, or have the greatness of cooking thrust upon her.

Bebe is probably head chef at New York's Four Seasons today.

Wherever she is, here are my recipes for beef Wellington, gazpacho, *petit pois*, twice-baked potatoes, and haricots verts.

Beef Wellington

2–3 pounds top tenderloin

Salt and freshly ground black pepper, to taste

1 small onion, minced

2 stalks celery, minced

2 portobello mushrooms, minced

2 tablespoons (¼ stick) butter

1 sheet Puffed Pastry (recipe follows)

½ pound chicken liver pâté

1 large egg

½ cup water

Preheat oven to 375°F.

Season tenderloin with salt and pepper, and roast for 45 minutes. Interior tenderloin temperature should be 135–145°F for medium. Remove from oven. Let cool. Reduce oven temperature to 325°F.

In large skillet, sauté onion, celery, mushrooms, and butter—this is called duxelles.

Take Puffed Pastry from refrigerator, and roll out on floured board. If pastry is too dry, add cold water sparingly. Sheet should measure 3 inches longer and 5 inches wider than roast. Place half the duxelles on pastry. Place roast on the duxelles mixture. Cover roast with pâté. Put the remaining duxelles on tops and sides of the roast. Bring pastry dough up to cover sides, ends, and top of the roast.

Mix egg and water together. With cooking brush, spread egg wash on sides, ends, and top of pastry. Bake for 40 minutes.

Puffed Pastry

2 cups sifted all-purpose flour
½ teaspoon baking powder
½ teaspoon salt
⅔ cup soft shortening
1 large egg, beaten with 2 tablespoons milk

Sift together flour, baking powder, and salt. Cut in shortening. Mix in egg mixture lightly. Chill for 1 hour.

Gazpacho

SERVES 6 TO 8

½ clove garlic, minced

1 teaspoon salt

3 tablespoons olive oil

3 tablespoons vinegar

2½ cups cold water

4 tomatoes, diced

2 cups canned tomato juice, chilled

1 green bell pepper, diced

2 tablespoons minced onion

1 cucumber, diced

2 stalks celery, diced

½ cup bread croutons

Blend garlic, salt, oil, vinegar, and water. Add tomatoes and tomato juice. Serve bell pepper, onion, cucumber, celery, and croutons on the side. Each person can choose veggies and croutons as desired.

Petit Pois

SERVES 4 TO 6

1 pound fresh small green peas
2 cups chicken stock or water
½ pound cooked pearl onions
Salt and freshly ground black
    pepper, to taste

2 tablespoons butter
2 tablespoons all-purpose flour
1 cup cold milk

In small, heavy pot, cook peas in stock over medium heat for 5 minutes. Add onions and cook another 5 minutes. Drain.

Season peas and onions with salt and pepper and butter. Mix flour with milk, then add to peas and onions, stirring quickly. Cook over medium heat, stirring constantly for 10 minutes. If cream sauce is too thick, add water to desired thinness.

Twice-Baked Potatoes

4 large Idaho baking potatoes

1 teaspoon vegetable oil

4 green onions (white and green parts), minced

1 cup sour cream

2 tablespoons (¼ stick) butter

Salt and freshly ground black pepper, to taste

½ cup grated white cheddar cheese

Preheat oven to 350°F.

Scrub and pat dry potatoes, and grease with oil. Bake for 45 minutes. Remove from oven, and increase oven temperature to 375°F.

When potatoes have cooled, cut lengthwise, and scrape center from potatoes carefully, leaving ⅛ inch so that walls of potatoes will not collapse. Mix remaining ingredients in bowl, and mash with potatoes. Divide mashed potatoes equally among shells. Bake for 30 minutes.

Haricots Verts

SERVES 6

2 pounds thin green beans	3 quarts water
½ teaspoon salt	Vinaigrette (recipe follows)

Cook beans over medium heat in salted water until crispy tender. Drain well, cool, and pour Vinaigrette over beans.

Vinaigrette

MAKES 1½ CUPS

½ cup water
1 cup cider vinegar
½ teaspoon dried tarragon
½ teaspoon dried thyme
3 tablespoons olive oil
1 clove garlic, minced
Salt, to taste

Bring water to boil. Add vinegar to water and scald for 5 minutes. Remove from heat, and cool. Add dried herbs, olive oil, and garlic, and season with salt.

Sisterly Translation

❧ ✦ ❧

R OSA GUY AND I BECAME GOOD FRIENDS in New York City during the late 1950s. She was Trinidadian-born and brought to the United States when she was seven years old. I had been born in Missouri and raised everywhere. Still, we had much in common. We were nearly the same age, enjoyed music, food, dancing, and relished the company of high-spirited men. We were both good cooks and admired each other's skills. She was a founding member of the Harlem Writers Guild, and because I also belonged to the association some other members tried to set up a cooking competition between us. We refused to be drawn into such an unproductive use of energy.

Rosa told me that Trinidadians make and eat souse during the Christmas and New Year's holidays. I told her that people in Stamps, Arkansas, where I grew up, do the same. She always invited friends to celebrate Thanksgiving at her house but now suggested that we might like to do New Year's at my apartment. She and I would both make souse to help celebrate. We would eat and then go to Central Park to drink champagne and watch fireworks.

New Year's Eve bloomed and Rosa arrived early with her souse. I confess to being a little nervous. My grandmother was the best cook I had ever known and I had used her recipe. Rosa set her bowl down on the kitchen table and lifted the top. I must have given a little scream.

She asked, "What's the matter?"

I said, "Those are pig's feet."

She said, "Yes, of course. It's souse."

I pulled my souse from the refrigerator and ran a knife around the side of the dish and unmolded the contents.

She asked, "What is that?"

I said, "Souse."

We looked at each other, then at our so different dishes. There was nothing for it but to laugh.

She asked, "You call that souse?"

"Everybody I know in Arkansas calls that souse and we call what you've got pickled pig's feet."

She said, "Of course you make souse out of pig's feet. Here, have a taste."

Her dish was wonderful. The skin on the pig's feet was white and there were rings of onion and wedges of crisp green peppers. I ate the piece she pulled off and it was exactly what we called pickled pig's feet.

I said, "Taste this." Then I took a slice from my loaf-molded souse.

She ate it. "That's good. That's hog head cheese."

I said, "Yes, but we also call it souse."

When the guests arrived, we served them hog head cheese and pig's feet and unending champagne.

When a person relished my dish, I would look over to Rosa and smirk. Each time her souse received a compliment, she would all but stick out her tongue at me. I imagined had we been alone and ten years old, she would have put both her hands behind her ears and moved them forward and I would have made a face and said, Nyah, nyah, nyah, nyah.

For many years we brought in the new year in Central Park with champagne after having eaten souse, hog head cheese, and pickled pig's feet in my apartment.

Pickled Pig's Feet, or Souse

SERVES 6

6 pig's feet

2 tablespoons salt

½ teaspoon freshly ground black pepper

2 cups cider vinegar (or more, to taste)

5 whole cloves

1 tablespoon sugar

1 teaspoon red pepper flakes

3 large green bell peppers, quartered

3 large onions, sliced into rings

Scrape and clean pig's feet. Place in large pot, and add boiling water to cover. Cook over medium heat until pig's feet are tender, about 4 hours. Add 1 tablespoon salt, ¼ teaspoon black pepper, 1 cup vinegar, 3 cloves, ½ tablespoon sugar, and ½ teaspoon red pepper flakes to broth. Cook 1 more hour.

Remove pig's feet from hot broth and cool.

Make another brine with remaining salt, black pepper, vinegar, cloves, sugar, and red pepper flakes. Boil 15 minutes, then cool. Pour over cooled pig's feet. Place in refrigerator. Add wedges of bell pepper and rings of onion to cold brine. Serve cold.

Hog Head Cheese

5 pounds pig's feet
1 pound pig's ears
2 pounds pork roast
1½ bottles Chardonnay
2 cups cider vinegar
1 large onion, studded with 6 cloves
8 stalks celery
5 bay leaves

10 black peppercorns
Five 1-ounce packages Knox gelatin
3 teaspoons salt
3 teaspoons freshly ground black
   pepper
2 red bell peppers
Cornichons (optional)

In large pot, place pig's feet, ears, and pork roast in wine and vinegar, and add enough water to cover. Place clove-studded onion, celery, bay leaves, and peppercorns in cheesecloth bag, and add to pot.

Mix gelatin in 2 cups cool water, and add to pot along with salt, pepper, and bell peppers. Bring to a boil, and simmer about 4 hours, skimming the surface as it cooks. Cool, then strain, reserving liquid. Carefully remove all bones.

Cut up pig's ears, meat from pig's feet, and pork roast. Place in large bowl, and mix well. Check seasoning and return strained liquid. Pour into 6 loaf pans, or more if needed. Cover with plastic wrap, and put into refrigerator for 5 or more hours. When cool and set, turn out of pans onto cutting board. Slice and serve like pâté. Place each slice on salad plate, and add a few cornichons if desired.

Dolly and Sherry and Making Sisters

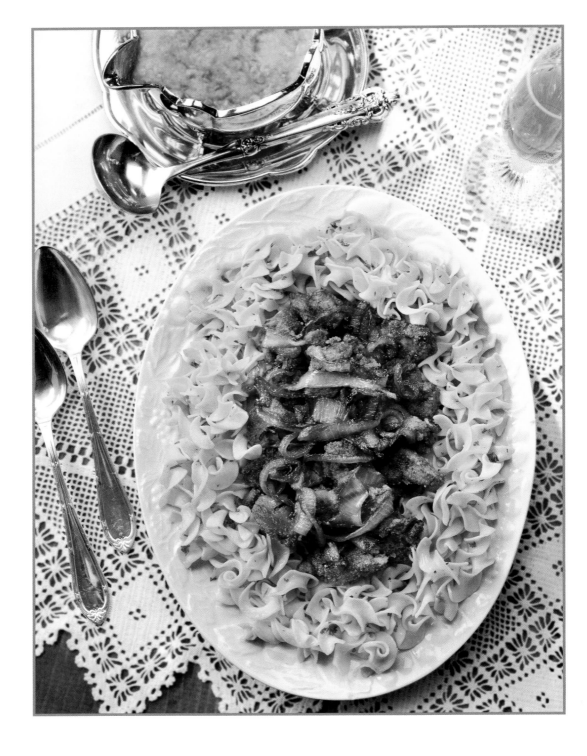

D OLLY MCPHERSON AND I MET at a party in Rosa Guy's home. Before she
left, she invited me to her house for brunch the next morning. She said the
invitation included Rosa. I thanked her and said I would come but that I wasn't
sure about Rosa. I knew that in Rosa's house, after a rough Saturday night, Sunday morning always came late and didn't come easily. To my surprise, Rosa said
yes, she would love to come. She wanted to see what someone so proper would
serve for brunch.

Dolly's apartment was ready to be photographed for *House Beautiful*. In the living room a Federal nineteenth-century sofa sat on a lilac wall-to-wall carpet. An
antique sewing table functioned as a side table while Queen Anne chairs sur-
rounded a Duncan Phyfe table. Her walls were filled with fine art. Dolly was
graced in a long housecoat. We had laughed together so quickly the night before
that I had not noticed her very formal manners.

She served us good sherry in beautiful crystal glasses. I complimented her on
their beauty and she said she had picked them up in France during her tour as a
Fulbright Scholar.

Had the aromas from the kitchen not burgeoned with savory promises, I
would have thought that maybe she was too highfalutin to cook for my taste.

I told her the food smelled inviting, then asked if she had some scotch. She
said yes, and when Rosa said she'd like scotch as well Dolly said she would join us
but with a sherry.

On her last trip from the kitchen, she announced that brunch was served.

Her dining table could have groaned under the weight of her offerings.
Parsleyed egg noodles shone under a lathering of butter, and in another dish

string beans looked crisp and pert. There was a loaf of warm bread on a cutting board and a lovely platter of sautéed chicken livers and onions. A gravy boat filled with dark brown sauce sat nearby.

It looked good enough to eat. I hoped it was. The livers earned my lifelong respect. They were well done but still soft, and the gravy was delicious without the well-known bitterness so often found in liver gravy. The beans were tender but still had some crunchy character, and the crust of the bread was crisp while the soft inside was warm enough to make the room-temperature butter submit.

Rosa smiled at the table with approval.

When we finished brunch, Dolly said now she would have a scotch. She liked to have a full meal before she drank liquor. That sounded reasonable to me.

On the strength of the perfectly cooked brunch and on the chemistry that passed between us, I thought I'd like to have Dolly for my sister-friend.

That was nearly forty years ago and we now live in the same town and each of us has spent decades working at the same university. We still say hallelujah for our sisterhood and I am still praising Dolly's chicken livers and gravy. And I have become used to having a sherry before dinner, with the meal, and a scotch after.

Chicken Livers

1 pound chicken livers
Salt and freshly ground black
   pepper, to taste
3/4 cup all-purpose flour
3 tablespoons vegetable oil
2 tablespoons diced celery

2 tablespoons minced green onion
   (white and green parts)
1 medium onion, finely diced
2 cups chicken broth
1/3 cup good-quality dry sherry

Wash and separate chicken livers, and pat dry. Season with salt and pepper, and dredge in 1/2 cup flour. Heat 2 tablespoons oil in large skillet, and sauté livers for 2 minutes on each side. Remove livers from skillet.

Add remaining oil to skillet, and sauté celery and all onions until translucent. Add remaining flour to skillet. When brown, add chicken broth. Cook for 3 minutes, stirring constantly. Put livers back in skillet, and add sherry. Cover, and cook for 5 minutes. Serve at once.

Buttered Noodles

1/2 teaspoon salt
2 quarts water
One 1-pound package egg noodles

2 tablespoons butter, softened
1 tablespoon finely chopped fresh
   parsley

In large pot, bring salted water to a boil. Add noodles. Cook over medium to high heat for 10 minutes, or until desired tenderness. Drain. Mix butter and parsley with noodles, and serve at once.

Writer's Block

THERE WERE BRICKS IN MY MATTRESS and rocks in my pillow and no rest at all in my bed. On the same lumpy surface my husband lay snoring gently, a look of sweet satisfaction on his face. I so envied his delicious peace that I was tempted to pinch the skin on his inner arm, but he deserved better treatment than that so I decided to get up and leave the bed and the indulgence of slumber to him. Stealthily I began to slide out of the bed. When my feet touched the floor, I pressed both hands on the mattress. I didn't want him to realize that I was getting up so I continued to press on the mattress releasing tension slowly until I could stand up straight and my husband could sleep on undisturbed.

I went into the kitchen and poured a glass of good Chardonnay. I had to confront the stress, which kept me from my rest. The truth was my writing was going badly. Or to put it directly, my writing was not going at all.

A sample of my work made me cry:

A RAT
SAT
ON A MAT
THAT'S THAT.

I was working on a fourth book, and although the others had been well received, it seemed to me this one would reveal to the world that I was a charlatan and couldn't write my way out of a brown paper sack.

I decided to cook a complicated dish, which would take my mind off the exacting task of writing. I chose to make chocolate éclairs with whipped cream and custard filling.

From the moment I decided to cook, I forgot about writing. Gone was my concern with nouns, pronouns, verbs, and dangling participles. I had made cream puffs and profiteroles before but never éclairs, so I had to concentrate.

I finished the dough and measured it for twelve éclairs. I decided to make six with custard filling and the rest filled with whipped cream. I turned on both ovens and put three éclairs on each cookie sheet and placed them on the middle rack of each oven. I made the custard and started the whipped cream.

I put a large block of unsweetened chocolate in the top of a double boiler and turned the fire low so the chocolate could melt.

When the oven whistle let me know that the pastries were done, I opened the oven door and nearly fainted. I had measured dough the size of six large cigars, three on each cookie sheet. They had grown into loaves the size of giant Italian bread. I took them out and put the next load into the oven and was handed back six more giant loaves.

While they cooled, I made more custard and more whipped cream and warmed more unsweetened chocolate. Hours passed as pastries cooled and custard thickened and cooled enough to be placed into the giant pastries. I dusted some of the giant pastries with powdered sugar and drizzled chocolate over them all. After stuffing the refrigerator in the kitchen full of them, I made room for them in the refrigerator outside by the swimming pool. Dawn had arrived bringing its pink and gold clouds before I was finished cooking and filling the éclairs.

When I went back to bed, I was exhausted. I felt as if I had made dessert for an army. When my husband awakened and turned to sit up on his side of the bed, I raised myself and sat up, pretending I had not lain down just one hour earlier.

When my husband sat down for his coffee, I asked, "Would you like a little chocolate éclair?" (I knew he loved sweet pastries in the morning.) I chopped off a huge piece from the custard loaf. "When did you make this?" He ate so happily I didn't feel the need to answer.

That evening after dinner I offered a whipped cream éclair. He said, "Of course." The next day we repeated the actions of the day before except that I gave him whipped cream for breakfast and custard for dinner. The next morning he awakened before I did and left the bedroom. He came back immediately.

"Maya, Maya, wake up. What the hell have we got? Come here."

I followed him to the kitchen. He opened the refrigerator door. Sliced éclairs were stacked on every shelf. He said, "Come outside." He opened the refrigerator door on the deck. "What the hell do we have? An éclair cottage industry?"

"Would you have a bite before you go to work?" I asked.

"No, no. And I'll never eat another éclair as long as I live. I want to see my plate éclair-free when I come home tonight. I know you are having a hard time at your work and I'm sorry. So give them away or you eat them, but I don't fancy dessert made on a crisis-control watch."

I gave most of the éclairs to friends, to staff, and to the soup kitchen at church. But I kept one gargantuan loaf as proof that cooking helps me to write.

I pulled out the stubborn manuscript, which to date had resisted me successfully, and suddenly the words spilled out of my pen and onto the yellow pad.

A few days after my husband had said he never wanted to see another éclair, I offered him a piece of strawberry shortcake. He smiled widely and enjoyed it immensely. He just did not recognize the old éclair simply smothered with strawberries and fresh whipped cream.

Éclairs

MAKES 16 ÉCLAIRS

1 cup water

8 tablespoons (1 stick) butter or
   margarine

1/4 teaspoon salt

1 cup sifted all-purpose flour

1/2 cup confectioners' sugar

4 large eggs, beaten individually

Custard Filling and/or Golden
   Whipped Cream (recipes follow)

Chocolate Syrup (recipe follows)

Preheat oven to 400°F.

In large saucepan, heat water, butter, and salt to full rolling boil. Reduce heat to low, and quickly stir in flour and confectioners' sugar, mixing vigorously with wooden spoon until mixture leaves the sides of the pan in a ball.

Remove from heat. Add eggs one at a time, beating after each addition until mixture is very smooth. (An electric mixer at a low speed makes this procedure easier.) Force mixture through pastry tube, or shape with spatula into 16 fingers, each 1 × 4 inches.

Bake on greased cookie sheets for 25 to 30 minutes. Remove at once to racks and let cool away from drafts.

Cut the pastries in half lengthwise, spoon onto the bottoms either Custard Filling or Golden Whipped Cream, and replace the tops. Drizzle Chocolate Syrup over the éclairs.

Custard Filling

FILLS 8 ÉCLAIRS

3 large eggs
¼ cup sugar
Dash of salt
2 cups milk
½ teaspoon vanilla extract

Beat eggs, sugar, salt, and milk until blended in top part of double boiler. Put over simmering water and cook, stirring, for about 7 minutes or until mixture thickens slightly and coats a metal spoon. Remove from hot water and pour into bowl. Add vanilla extract. Cool and chill 1 hour.

Golden Whipped Cream

FILLS 8 ÉCLAIRS

2 cups whipping cream
⅔ cup brown sugar
½ teaspoon vanilla extract

Whip cream until it holds peaks. Gradually add brown sugar and vanilla extract. Cool and chill 1 hour.

Chocolate Syrup

6 ounces (6 squares) unsweetened chocolate, melted, or 1 cup cocoa
1½ cups sugar
⅛ teaspoon salt
1 cup boiling water
½ teaspoon vanilla extract

In small saucepan, mix melted chocolate with sugar and salt over low heat. Add boiling water, and cook for 5 minutes, stirring constantly. Cool, add vanilla extract, and refrigerate.

Massachusetts, Tennessee, and an Italian Soup

A GROUP OF TEACHERS of foreign languages met in Nashville, Tennessee. The Opryland Hotel was the site of the conference.

The corridors spiking out from the large meeting hall were filled with conversations in Spanish, French, Italian, Japanese, Russian, and some languages I could not recognize.

I had been the morning lecturer and had spoken on the impossibility of successfully translating poetry, yet the imperative that we continue to attempt its translation. The lecture had been well received.

Afterward my assistant and I headed for a restaurant in the hotel. We found a table and ordered coffee. I am much easier to get along with after a few cups of coffee.

Two couples at the next table recognized me, and we began a light and friendly conversation. They were teachers from Springfield, Massachusetts, but had not been a part of the morning's conference. The couples explained that they were best of friends in Massachusetts and that they loved the Opryland Hotel and came on vacation together once a year.

One of the women waved her hands around in the air. "Have you ever seen anything like this?"

I admitted that I had not. It was kitsch at its best and had enough elegance to ward off derision. It was one of the largest hotels in the world. Huge fountains of water arched and fell, dancing to music of Bizet and Hayden. Flowers waved everywhere and restaurants rotated slowly while multicolored birds sang.

Doris, at the next table, said, "But don't order the minestrone. Never order the minestrone."

She said the four of them were Italian Americans and her husband had a rule. If he had had a little too much wine the night before, he liked a hot bowl of minestrone the next day to set him straight. She said he had just ordered it.

"Look at what they served him."

She tilted a soup bowl for me to see. The contents of his bowl looked like cooked oatmeal.

Doris said, "Looks like oatmeal, doesn't it?"

I said, "Yes."

She said, "We'll be back next year, but we just won't order their minestrone."

As soon as she said good-bye, a very trim and handsome young black man came to my table. "Dr. Angelou, we are so honored to have you here in this dining room. Let me introduce myself. I am the manager. Can we do anything for you?"

I said, "No, thank you."

He said, "I want to bring Mr. Williams, he is my manager and manager of the other restaurants here. He'll be so glad to welcome you."

I had finished breakfast, but courtesy kept me in my seat.

The young man returned with an older, elegant black man. He was introduced.

The man said, "We are honored and would love to have you visit some of the larger restaurants, but would you please come to this kitchen and let the workers see you. They will be thrilled."

I followed him into the kitchen, met and shook hands with everyone. My host said, "Now, this is the steam table. Here we keep food hot that has already been cooked."

I looked into the pots. One was filled with something like oatmeal. The contents were so thick, the ladle stood straight in its middle.

I asked, "And what is this?"

He said, "Oh, that's Minnesota wild rice. It's very popular at lunchtime, but they even had a call for it this morning at breakfast."

Indeed. That was what the woman at the next table had showed me. My impulse was to tell him that my friends from Springfield, Massachusetts, had not meant to order Minnesota wild rice and that maybe what he needed was a good recipe for minestrone for those who might want it on a given morning. I could have suggested that his Tennessee waiters' ears had misunderstood accents from New England and that New England ears did not completely understand Tennessee drawl, but Mr. Williams's smile was so nice and his attitude so welcoming, I didn't have the heart.

Minestrone Soup

MAKES 2 QUARTS

1 cup dried lima beans
2 quarts water
¼ cup olive oil
3 stalks celery, diced
1 medium onion, minced
One 19-ounce can crushed tomatoes
2 cups shredded cabbage
2 garlic cloves, minced
1 teaspoon salt

¼ teaspoon freshly ground black pepper
1 teaspoon chopped fresh parsley
½ teaspoon dried basil
½ teaspoon dried oregano
½ cup (dry measure) elbow macaroni, cooked al dente
Grated Parmesan cheese

Pick over beans, discarding stones and debris. Wash and drain, then put in large pot with water to cover, bring to boil, and boil for 2 minutes. Let cool for 2 hours.

Heat oil in large skillet, and lightly sauté celery, onion, tomatoes, cabbage, and garlic. Add to beans along with salt, pepper, and herbs. Cook covered, over medium heat, for 2 to 3 hours.

Before serving, pour cooked macaroni into soup. Bring to a boil, and boil for 4 minutes. Serve garnished with Parmesan.

Minnesota Wild Rice

1 cup uncooked wild rice
2 cups chicken stock
½ teaspoon salt
1 teaspoon minced onion

4 tablespoons (½ stick) butter
¼ teaspoon freshly ground black
pepper

Wash rice, drain, and cover with water. Bring to a boil, then reduce heat to low immediately. After 20 minutes, add 1 cup of water, and cook for another 20 minutes. Then rinse and drain again. Pour in chicken stock. Add salt, onion, butter, and pepper. Simmer covered until tender and all liquid has evaporated, about 45 minutes.

Black Iron
Pot Roast

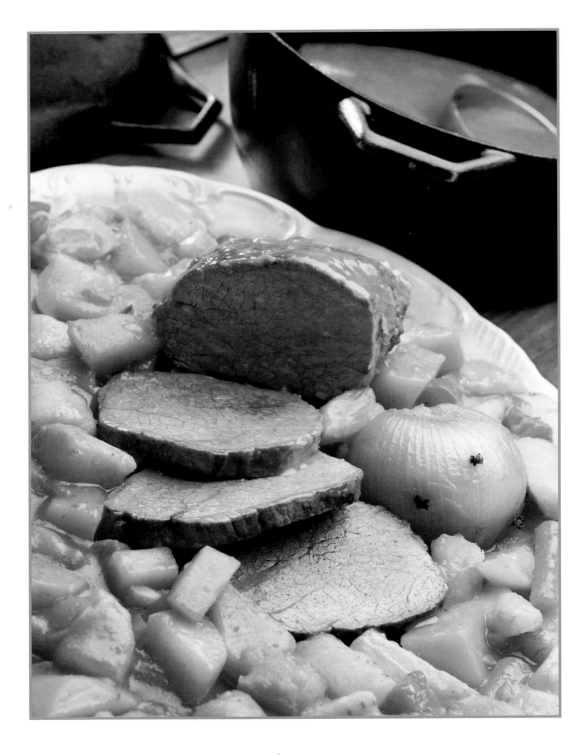

ᆬ᥉ ✦ ᥉ᆬ

LEE GOLDSMITH OWNED a chic cookery store on New York's Upper West Side. She was a striking woman with a sharp wit who knew a lot about cooking. I often found myself in her store either buying a cooking tool or just talking about food and its preparation.

I passed her shop one morning, and through the window I saw her perched on a stool, bent over, her head in her hands and her shoulders heaving. Obviously she was crying. I opened the door.

"What's the matter?"

She did not lift her head.

"Lee, what's the matter?"

She sat up and I saw tears on her face. I also recognized that she wasn't crying. She was caught up in paroxysms of laughter.

I had to wait until she could find and hold a full breath of air. Finally, after many false starts, she said, "A customer came in here, cursed me out, and said she was going to sue me."

Here, laughter took over her again so completely that her body shook.

The story came out in pieces between laughing interruptions.

The woman had come two days earlier and asked if Lee had a heavy black pot for sale. She showed her the item.

The woman asked, "Could you cook a pot roast in this? I have a recipe that I had to steal to get." When Lee answered in the affirmative, the customer asked, "How do you use the pot? Do I have to wash it first?"

Lee explained that any pots or pans sent from a factory must be scrubbed thoroughly to remove a film, which is put on to prevent rust.

The customer asked, "I should wash it?"

Lee said, "Get a Brasso scourer, use a little Ajax, and scrub the pot inside and out. Wash the pot again, and then use Brillo soap pads to scrub it again. When it feels smooth, wash it with regular dish-washing liquid. Dry it with a soft towel. Put some vegetable oil on your hands. Rub that all over the pot and the lid. Put the two into a very slow oven, about 150°F, overnight. Next morning, take it out, let it cool, wash it again lightly, and then continue with your pot roast recipe."

I told Lee that sounded about right. She said yes, except that the customer came into the shop screaming, "You have ruined my life. I followed your instructions and my fiancé brought his parents for dinner last night. His mother makes a killer pot roast and I paid somebody to get her recipe for me. I followed hers as I followed yours, but when I served it they all began to frown and then giggle, and finally they all started laughing. Some of them said they had to pick steel wool out of their teeth."

Lee asked the woman how she had prepared the pot roast.

The customer said, "I did what you suggested. I took the meat and scrubbed with a brass scourer and Ajax. Then I washed it and dried it and washed it again with a soapy Brillo pad. I washed it finally with dish-washing liquid and patted it dry. I put the oil on my hands and rubbed it and put it in a low oven, 150°F, overnight. Yesterday morning I took it out of the oven, and when it was cooled I washed it again and then followed my pot roast recipe.

"I served it last night and they laughed so hard, I put them out of my house— my fiancé and his parents and some friends they had brought with them.

"I'm on my way to send my ring back to the jerk. I never want to hear his name again."

Lee said, "Wait at least a day. No, better wait a week. Do you love him?"

The customer started crying. "Yes."

"Then wait a week. If you can bear to see him, bring him here and I will explain how we miscommunicated." The customer dried her eyes and was a little mollified and said, "I'll think about it. But if I can't forgive him, believe me, I won't forgive you. I will sue your ass."

When Lee and I stopped laughing, she invited me over to her house for pot roast. Hers was delicious.

Black Iron Pot Roast

5–6 pounds rolled boneless beef chuck

Salt and freshly ground black pepper, to taste

3 tablespoons all-purpose flour

1 tablespoon vegetable oil

1 large onion, studded with 5 cloves

3 carrots, peeled and cut into large pieces

1 stalk celery, cut into large pieces

1 cup water or beef stock

3 tablespoons cornstarch mixed with 3 tablespoons water

Preheat oven to 350°F.

Season meat with salt and pepper; then dust lightly with flour.

In Dutch oven with tight-fitting cover, brown meat slowly on all sides in hot oil.

Add onion, carrots, celery, and water.

Cover tightly, and bake for 2 hours, or until meat is very tender. Check pot every half hour, adding water if needed. Do not allow meat to burn.

Remove meat. Thicken liquid with a cornstarch-and-water paste for gravy. Serve with boiled and buttered potatoes.

Oprah's Suffocated Chicken

I GAVE A SERIES OF SEMINARS at a university in Maryland. On my last day, a fifth request for an interview was about to receive the same negative response I had given the other four.

"I appreciate the request, but I have a plane to catch . . ."

The voice said, "Doctor, I only need five minutes of your time. You have my word you will be free to go in five minutes." She sounded so cool and definite.

I asked, "Do you want me to come to your studio?"

"No, Dr. Angelou, I will bring my crew to you and I won't disturb you until we are set up and I am ready to shoot. I give you my word."

I was won over. Anybody can find five minutes in a day despite its other demands. The reporter told me her name, but it didn't catch in my memory. I said yes and gave her a time.

When I informed my host at the university that I had agreed to give an interview, he asked why after having refused the other requests. I answered, "I rarely find young people today (and she sounds young) who know that one's word is a powerful thing and that it can be given or it can be withheld." That television journalist had impressed me enough to make me curious to see how good her word was.

The next day when I concluded my seminar, an attractive young woman opened the classroom door.

"Dr. Angelou?"

"Yes."

"I am here to do the interview. My crew is set up. We are ready if you are!"

I followed her to the next room and she pointed out a chair. She had put a pillow in the chair so that the camera could be level to my face. I sat. She looked at her watch and automatically I looked at mine. She nodded and the crew leapt to attention. She asked one question, and I was so surprised at its complexity and relevance that it engaged my total attention. She really listened to my answer and her second question stemmed from my response.

She looked at her watch and said, "Thank you, Dr. Angelou."

My watch told me that exactly five minutes had passed.

I told her that because of our hurried telephone conversation the day before I had not really caught her name.

She said, "Oprah Winfrey."

I said, "Young woman, you will go far. I hope to be around to see your success."

A few years later I attended a social affair in Chicago and I saw her standing on the side. I walked over and said, "Hello, Oprah Winfrey. How are you?"

She said, "You remember me, and you remembered my name."

I said, "Of course. You are going to do wonderful things in your lifetime."

She had been offered her own show in Chicago and had accepted. She knew that Phil Donahue was the most popular daytime host in the nation and that he also broadcasted from Chicago. Donahue would be formidable competition.

I gave her my card and invited her to come and visit me in North Carolina.

One month later, she came and brought her gentleman friend. I served smothered chicken and rice, which was well received.

After dinner the first night we sat on the floor and read poetry. Her delight in the beauty of the spoken word pleased me. I told her that all poetry was music written for the human voice. We recited long into the night.

The next morning as I was planning breakfast for my houseguests, she came pajamaed into the kitchen.

She said, "Your house feels like home."

I said, "I hope you will always think that."

I told her that the poet Robert Frost had said, "Home is where when you go there, no one can put you out."

I said, "I offer you this home whenever you need it or even if you just want it.

"Would you like eggs and bacon? Grits and sausage? Ham and green tomatoes?"

She laughed and said she'd like some of the previous night's dinner of chicken and biscuits.

At the table she asked, "What do you call this dish?" She pointed to the chicken.

I said, "That's smothered chicken."

She said, "No, this is too good for such a simple name. This is suffocated chicken." She then added, "This chicken never knew what hit it."

Smothered Chicken

SERVES 8

Two 3-pound fryer chickens
Juice of 2 lemons
½ teaspoon salt
½ teaspoon freshly ground black
    pepper
1 cup all-purpose flour

8 tablespoons (1 stick) butter
½ cup vegetable oil
2 medium onions, sliced
1 pound button mushrooms, sliced
1 clove garlic, minced
2 cups chicken broth

Wash and pat dry chicken. Cut into pieces, and put in a bowl with lemon juice and water to cover. Refrigerate for 1 hour.

Wash lemon water off chicken, and season with salt and pepper. Dredge pieces in ³/₄ cup flour.

In large skillet, fry chicken parts on high heat in butter and ¹/₄ cup oil until dark brown. Remove from skillet.

Add remaining flour and oil to skillet. Cook flour until brown. Add onions, mushrooms, and garlic, stirring constantly. Put chicken back into skillet. Add chicken broth and water to cover. Turn heat to medium, and cook for 25 minutes.

Serve with Buttermilk Biscuits (p. 41).

Ashford
Salad '96

A DINNER WITHOUT MEAT can satisfy. Prepared with skill, it can even delight. But I did not know that when I was a child. I grew up during an impoverished time and in a poor part of the United States.

The Depression, which assailed the entire country, hit the South with a particularly heavy blow. Poor people who lived in a cotton economy and who were happy to have fresh meat once a month were challenged to find enough work to put the sparest vegetarian dinners on their tables.

Those who were used to eating fresh meat at least twice a week were challenged to find the resources to buy it twice a month.

I belonged to the first group, and although we did have chickens and cured meat, vegetables dominated our meals, whether we wished it or not. Inventive cooks found ways to use the cured meat that was included in their cooked dishes. Each pot of greens was stewed with as much smoked or cured meat as the cook could afford. Country ham slices and boiled bacon slabs were offered at least once a week, and one could be assured that it was definitely chicken on Sunday.

After I grew up and away from the days of poverty and the southern place of need, I found that I often wished for a meatless dinner of crunchy vegetables and an oven-roasted Irish potato, or pasta with a fresh tomato sauce. However, until I met Valerie Simpson and Nick Ashford I had never thought it could be exciting to be creative in cooking vegetarian food. The songwriting couple came to visit me in North Carolina, and within hours they had taken my heart. I could think of nothing more pleasing than to please them. Valerie would eat chicken and fish, but Nick was a definite vegetarian. I bought the prepared dishes made of soybeans from the supermarket. They were concocted of mushrooms and oats and rice. I tasted them and they were horrible. I decided I would simply try to cook vegetables so well that the diner would prefer my dish to a standing rib roast. I know that was wishful thinking but I also knew that good veggies well prepared could please any palate.

First I offered a dish called *chakchouka* in North Africa and *ratatouille* in France. Then I served a tomato soufflé with snow peas and celery gratin as side dishes. Nick loved it. One day I offered a salad that Nick liked so much I named it the Ashford '96.

When I served another mixed salad with feta and golden raisins, not only did Nick decide that I was one of the best cooks he had ever known, he had to know the exact measurements in all my salad recipes.

The Ashford-Simpsons were a bright and beautiful couple, quick and funny, and I had long admired their talent, but their shared laughter, love, and gentle personalities won them to my heart. I gave the recipes to them a number of times, but they swore they could not replicate the dishes.

When they visit me in North Carolina and when I go see them in New York, they look at me with such large, longing eyes that without being asked I will go to the kitchen and make one of "Nick's green salads."

Here are the recipes for the salads and other vegetarian dishes I created for Nick Ashford.

Tomato Soufflé

Three 28-ounce cans crushed
  tomatoes
5 tablespoons butter
½ teaspoon sugar
½ teaspoon salt, plus pinch
4 slices white bread, torn into
  medium-size pieces

2 tablespoons all-purpose flour
1 teaspoon cornstarch
1 cup cold milk
5 large eggs, separated

Sauté tomatoes in large skillet with 2 tablespoons butter, sugar, and ¼ teaspoon salt until dry. Add bread, and mix well. Cool.

Preheat oven to 350°F.

Use 1 tablespoon butter to grease soufflé dish. Sprinkle ¼ teaspoon salt in soufflé dish so that it coats bottom and sides.

Melt remaining butter in large saucepan over medium heat. Add flour and cornstarch, and stir for 1 minute. Add milk all at once. Stir. Remove from heat. Add egg yolks into mixture one at a time. Add sautéed tomatoes, mixing well.

In a clean, dry bowl, beat whites of eggs with pinch of salt until stiff. Fold into soufflé mixture carefully. Pour mixture into soufflé dish, filling it three-quarters full. Bake for 35 minutes, or until puffed and golden. Serve immediately.

Chakchouka

(Moroccan stew)

SERVES 8 TO 10

6 tablespoons olive oil

2 large eggplants, peeled and cut into 2-inch pieces

1 large onion, sliced

2 green bell peppers, cut into large pieces

1 red bell pepper, cut into large pieces

2 zucchini, cut into large pieces

2 yellow squash, cut into large pieces

4 tomatoes, peeled and chopped

4 cloves garlic, minced

Salt and freshly ground black pepper, to taste

Heat oil in large, heavy pot. Add eggplant, and fry for 4 to 5 minutes. Add onion, and sauté until translucent. Add remaining ingredients, cover, and stir over medium-low heat for 25 minutes. Check seasonings and adjust if needed.

Ashford Salad '96

SERVES 6 TO 8

2 heads romaine lettuce, with tough
    outer leaves removed

4 tablespoons extra-virgin olive oil

3 tablespoons fresh lemon juice

2 tablespoons red wine vinegar

1 tablespoon sugar

2 cloves garlic, finely minced

Salt and freshly ground black
    pepper, to taste

1 ripe avocado, peeled and diced

1 large ripe tomato, cut into small
    wedges

1 large English cucumber, sliced

Wash lettuce, dry, wrap in paper towels, and put into refrigerator. Mix oil, lemon juice, vinegar, sugar, and garlic in large salad bowl. Season with salt and pepper. Mash avocado with potato masher, and mix with ingredients in salad bowl. Check seasonings. Mix in tomato and cucumber. Just before serving, remove lettuce from refrigerator. Break into large pieces, and toss into salad bowl. With salad tongs, mix vigorously until each lettuce leaf has been flavored with dressing.

Mixed Salad with Feta and Golden Raisins

SERVES 4

1 head Bibb lettuce

1 bunch watercress

1 cup golden raisins

2 tablespoons extra-virgin olive oil

3 tablespoons fresh lemon juice

½ tablespoon balsamic vinegar

1 teaspoon finely minced fresh garlic

Salt and freshly ground black pepper, to taste

1 cup crumbled feta cheese

Remove and discard old leaves from lettuce and watercress; then wash. Wrap in paper towels and refrigerate. Put raisins into small pot with water to cover, and simmer for 3 minutes. Take off heat and set aside so raisins can plump. In large salad bowl, place oil, lemon juice, vinegar, and garlic. Season with salt and pepper. Mix well. Just before serving, remove greens from refrigerator, and tear into large pieces. Drain raisins, discarding water. Mix dressing and raisins and greens, and sprinkle feta cheese on top. Serve at once.

Index

⤜✦⤛

About the Author

Poet, writer, performer, teacher, and director MAYA ANGELOU was raised in Stamps, Arkansas, and then went to San Francisco. In addition to her bestselling autobiographies, beginning with *I Know Why the Caged Bird Sings*, she has also written five poetry collections, including *I Shall Not Be Moved* and *Shaker, Why Don't You Sing?*, as well as the celebrated poem "On the Pulse of Morning," which she read at the inauguration of President William Jefferson Clinton; "A Brave and Startling Truth," written at the request of the United Nations and read at its fiftieth anniversary; and "Amazing Peace," which she read at the lighting of the National Christmas Tree in Washington, D.C., in December 2005.

About the Type

Jenson is one of the earliest print typefaces. After hearing of the invention of printing in 1458, Charles VII of France sent coin engraver Nicolas Jenson to study this new art. Not long after, Jenson started a new career in Venice in letter-founding and printing. In 1471, Jenson was the first to present the form and proportion of this roman font that bears his name.

More than five centuries later, Robert Slimbach, developing fonts for the Adobe Originals program, created Adobe Jenson based on Nicolas Jenson's Venetian Renaissance typeface. It is a dignified font with graceful and balanced strokes.